BUT I HAVE CALLED YOU FRIENDS

BUT I HAVE CALLED YOU FRIENDS

Reflections on the Art of Christian Friendship

by

MOTHER MARY FRANCIS, P.C.C.

IGNATIUS PRESS   SAN FRANCISCO

Cover art: *The Last Supper* by Duccio (ca. 1260–1319)
Museo dell'Opera Metropolitana, Siena, Italy
Scala/Art Resource, N.Y.

Cover design by Riz Boncan Marsella

ISBN 978-1-58617-080-6
ISBN 1-58617-080-5
Library of Congress Control Number 2006921888
Printed in the United States of America ∞

In Memory of

our friend

Andrée Emery

CONTENTS

FOREWORD

In the early afternoon of February 11, 2006, the feast of Our Lady of Lourdes, the vibrant soul of Mother Mary Francis of Our Lady departed the worn-out little body that had housed it for nearly eighty-five years. Mother had a genius for friendship, as each of the twenty-five weeping Poor Clares who surrounded her bed in the small monastery infirmary could testify. We who had been privileged to watch in turn around her bed for nearly two months experienced the bonds of love deepening each day as she communicated her love and gratitude by word, by facial expression, by gesture, by snatches of song. Each sister felt herself to be very personally known, appreciated and cherished by Mother, and each one felt herself to be one of Mother's dearest friends. And, wonderful to tell, each one was.

Mother Mary Francis served as abbess of the Poor Clare Monastery of Our Lady of Guadalupe for forty-one years. During those years she also founded or restored six other monasteries, wrote numerous books, plays, and articles as well as several volumes of poetry. Through her writings and a vast correspondence, she encouraged religious on every continent to preserve the ideals of authentic religious life that were threatened by too-sweeping changes after the Second Vatican Council. In the course of her long, loving and immensely fruitful life she made an astounding number of friends.

After news of Mother's death spread, we were nearly over-whelmed with letters from her friends. Classmates who had studied with her more than sixty years ago had remained close by correspondence. Poor Clares and other religious from around the world had been writing to her for twenty, thirty, forty years. Cardinals, bishops, priests; a forest ranger in Montana; an architect in Illinois; a schoolteacher in Texas—all mourned the loss of a most dear friend. And each friendship had been unique, deep, true, and enduring.

The conferences in this small book were given to the novitiate sisters of the Roswell monastery in the late 1960s and early 1970s, but they do not apply exclusively to that fortunate audience. Mother Francis explores, in her gentle, humorous, and informal way, the timeless principles of friend-ship that help anyone who seeks a deepened understanding of the mystery of loving and being loved.

> Mother Mary Angela, P.C.C. (Abbess)
> Poor Clare Monastery of Our Lady of Guadalupe
> Roswell, New Mexico
> May 2006

I

The Common Denominator:
Simple and Demanding

Dear sisters, what I want to talk about this morning is friendship. This is about the oldest topic in the world. I think that in our era it is also the newest topic. It is the "in" subject. It seems that the Church and the world have discovered a need for friendship and decided that there is much to this business of friendship and fraternity. This is so characteristic of our present time. I think this is one of those areas where we could sit back and smile a little over this great new idea—two thousand years old. For I seem to remember that our dear Lord had quite a lot to say about fraternal love, and that he said it very plainly. It is at the very heart of his message that we should love one another. So, if we have lost the impact of his message, it is a very good thing that we are rediscovering it and experiencing the vibrations. Only let's not take it to ourselves as the discovery of our generation, because it has a lot of deep roots in Christian history, as everything being rediscovered in these exhilarating times has.

We want to talk about this over a period of some time because it is so important. And if it has been forgotten in society at large, then we have to admit that it sometimes has been a little overlooked (or maybe quite a lot over-looked) in religious life also. Now, friendship is the common denominator for every kind of love there is. I think that is the first thing I would like you to think about. There is no real love of any kind that is not rooted in friendship; and when love does not seem to be functioning properly, when it is not fruitful, it is always because there is not friendship in love. You see what is wrong with a lot of marriages. Too often people live in the marriage relationship and don't even like each other, and we know that this is the big problem that wrecks marriages. Two people who live so intimately really do not like each other, do not even have a love of friendship. Well, what are we going to base marriage on? The mere physical relationship won't hold up. It alone is not going to help these two people mature or help them be what God wants them to be.

It is the same with the love of a mother and her children. There has to be the love of friendship there. She isn't just the provider, the arbiter on occasion, the authority figure. Even in her authority status with her children, there has to be the element of friendship, for the love of a mother radiates out of this.

Now, in religious life we can't have sisters who are not friends. We can't have a superior and spiritual daughters who are not friends. And this is where relationships in religious life have bogged down and not fructified and not developed. We have a group of women living together with a common spiritual ideal, but not really knowing one another, not really with each other. We cannot call these people sisters. They may be associates in a common endeavor. But we cannot build religious life on that. Our Lord said, "I will not call you servants; I have called you friends" (Jn 15:15). And if we do not call each other friends, then let us not pretend that we can call each other sisters. We cannot have real sisters who are not real friends. And so it goes with every human relationship in life.

When a woman deliberately, for the love of God, cuts off, as it were, certain avenues of the expression of her love, something has to be done to divert the energy of that love into other channels. Therefore people who live as we live, consecrated women, consecrated virgins who have freely deprived themselves of the expression of love that is proper to marriage, that is proper to motherhood, must give all the riches of this love over into the channel of pure friendship. Friendship for one another, friendship for superiors, friendship for God, and therefore friendship with the world. So what is the conclusion? That we should be the experts in friendship. The religious community ought to be the pattern of friendship for the world. And because of the closeness of our life lived in community, lived in a cloister, we should have expertise in friendship. We ought to be the ones to whom other people could look for the clear picture of how real friendships work: this is the way it functions, this is what it does, this is what it produces in people.

There are a lot of ways we could define friendship, but I think it might be more helpful first to think about its three elements. They are esteem, respect, and affection. Now sometimes we have pseudofriendships or quasi-friendships, which don't hold up in real life. And often this is because we have got the elements in the wrong place. You feel an affection for someone or for certain people, and it is simply based on superficial elements. You don't really esteem that person; you don't really respect that person; and so the affection you feel for that person is a very thin kind of thing.

A genuine, lasting affection must spring from esteem and respect. We have to have a certain progression there.

There is an interesting point I would like to bring in here. Maybe you have thought of it. Have you ever reflected on the etymology of the word "respect"? Well, what do we have in the Latin *re* and *spectare*? We have *spectare*, "to look", and *re*, "again". The real meaning of the word "respect" is "to look again"; and I say more particularly to look again and again. When we do not have friendships with people, this is basically the reason. We haven't looked again and, very specifically, we haven't looked again and again and maybe *again*. Often we do not like the first look when we look at people, and so—that's it. We just turn off and decide, without pondering deeply. We have an unfortunate psychological reflex in this area: we look once, say "no like", and decide, without reasoning about it, of course, that we will have a different kind of relationship than friendship with this person.

This is a person we live with, yes; but we didn't like the first look, so we do not bother about this person or really get to know this person. And what do we usually mean when we say that we don't like a person? It is that we don't like something *about* that person; possibly we don't like quite a few things about that person. But I think that we should be very careful about allowing ourselves to admit to ourselves that we don't like a *person*.

If we feel dislike for other people, let us back ourselves into a corner and ask ourselves, why? You will probably find out that you don't like a certain thing about a person. It is a very salutary exercise because it is humiliating when we must admit what we don't like about that person. Sometimes it is the most ridiculous thing. Perhaps we don't like the register of her speaking voice. If her voice is too high-pitched or is full of gravel and gets on our nerves, especially when we are in a certain kind of mood and we're already nervous ourselves, we can feel a furious dislike for this person's tone of voice, and we can get all mixed up and think we dislike this person. We can start taking all kinds of measures that certain types of old "spiritual" books urge us to take. You know the kind of thing I mean: that we have to set our jaw and establish a "Christian relationship" with this person and kind of "offer her up" and any number of things as foolish and degrading as that. We don't like the way a person walks. Or perhaps someone has no rhythm at all or a very defective sense of rhythm. It can annoy us in the way she chants. "Why can't she catch on to the singing?" We can get so annoyed about these things that we think we don't like this person. We don't like her reactions to things. We don't like one person's insensitiveness; we don't like another person's sensitiveness. We have a whole dreary catalogue whereby we think we establish likes and dislikes.

Now all this is amusing in one sense. But you know, it is frightfully sad in another sense, because we can fail ever to get to know people once we have decided that we don't like them and that we must live with them on a different level. We judge that we cannot have a relationship of friendship with these people, and we simply do not look again. We have been so superficial that we have not looked past the things that annoy us and found out who this other person is, what she is all about, what she is like. This is what Charles Lamb meant when he made his famous assertion that it is impossible to dislike anyone whom we really know. That is quite a staggering statement, and it has been challenged by some; but I believe it. Think about it, think about it a great deal. Someone you really know, you cannot dislike. The trouble is that we think that we know people, and we really don't know them at all. So we must look again and again and then again; and gradually we shall get to know these people.

Something that we shall also go into later in more detail is that when we are looking again, we are not peering. More specifically, we are not shaking people by the shoulders trying to understand them (not literally, of course, but you know what I mean). You want to remember that this is a hazard for fervent souls. You take a conference like this very much to heart, and you are going to go into this thing, and you are going to understand your sisters—even if they die in the process! You are going to sort of lower your head and charge through everybody's doors. You are going to understand this person: what makes her tick; what sort of person she is. And this, of course, is perfectly deadly. This is a form of the do-it-yourself psychology that we definitely do not want to indulge in.

Understanding is a thing that grows, and it grows very slowly. We have to be patient. That is why I say, look again and again and *again*. Don't think, "I am going to understand this person today or in ten easy lessons." For one thing, we shall never completely understand another person. This is part of the wonder of Christ, the wonder of heaven, the wonder of God. It is only by God that any of us is completely understood; so don't try to fool yourself with the attitude: "I am going to understand you, even if it kills both of us (especially you)."

Now, I said that there are these three elements in friendship: esteem, respect, and affection. There are also two activities going on all the time in friendship, and they are interactive. One is the recognition of my friend's potential, and the other is the realization of my own. However, if I would ever enter into a consideration, even a theoretical consideration, of friendship as a development of my own potential, I am not setting out on the road to friendship. People are not instruments to be used or manipulated for my own ends; they are persons to be loved and understood. But when we are friends with people, then we really are realizing our own potential as well as helping them to realize theirs without pausing to cogitate on it at all.

Let us look at community life. How much do you find out about yourself in your relationships with other people? Quite a bit! And often quite a bit you'd much prefer not to have found out. If you lived by yourself, you wouldn't get this knowledge; you could die without it. I think this is why, according to all the old monastic rules, no one was permitted to live as a hermit until he had excelled in community life. And this doesn't mean that the person had just lived in community life, but that he had been outstanding in it. That he was "the man of the year", you might say, in community living. Then this person who appeared to have a specific call from God to live as a hermit might be allowed by the abbot to do so. Some Poor Clares have suggested that there might be a possibility of this in our lives. Well, if you feel that you want to live out in Saint Christopher's shed all by yourself and have trays brought to you, you've got to excel in community life before I'll even consider it! But whether you do that or not—and I haven't had any applicants yet—I want you to excel in community life.

This is it, dear sisters. This is the old, old idea our Lord had. We know the words so well, we know them as well as our own name, maybe better. But as with so many familiar things, we might not understand them because they are too simple. We are much better at understanding complex things than simple things. Simple things are much too demanding. And he did say, didn't he, that "by *this* all men will know that you belong to me, if you love one another" (Jn 13:35).

Well, this doesn't mean that we obviously belong to Jesus—we are religious; and so this was his directive for the laity. No, he decidedly meant this for religious, too. He meant us. He did not mean our relatives at home or the girls we went to college with, and for whom we agree it is an excellent gauge of Christianity. He meant it for us. I think this is a terrifying thought, that he might have to look at some religious and say, "They are not mine, because this one thing that I set up as a standard for recognizing who are mine, isn't there. These people do not love one another."

Well, my goodness, you say, that is out of the question! Of course we love one another! We wish each other well. We want everyone to go to heaven and live happily ever after with God and the rest of us. But we know that our Lord did not mean a generic love, a universalistic love. Yes, a love for everybody; but how can we have a universal love except by particularities? I have quoted to you before that famous sentence of Father R. H. J. Steuart's about love: that charity isn't a matter of opening a window on the world and saying, "I love the lot of you!" That's easy, but the trouble with it is that it isn't love. It is just benevolence, and it could become philanthropy; but it isn't really love because love is of its nature particular.

This takes us to particular friendships. That "particular friendship" that used to be written about and talked about to religious as though it were a dread and darksome thing. And it was mentioned in such a foreboding tone, often by retreat masters, that you felt this wasn't anything that you should ask your superior about. This was something too bad to be mentioned. It was said in hushed tones, "Beware of the particular friendship." Of course, I really had no idea when I entered religious life what was really meant in the darkest sense of the term: a perversion, a perverted "love".

But even without developing any element like this in our conference, what would a friendship be, I'd like to know, except particular? It is the very nature of friendship to be particular. We ought to have a particular relationship with every sister in the community. Why throw young religious into a panic about friendship and leave them to wonder the rest of their lives what kind of friendship they are supposed to have and possibly end up with none because they are not supposed to have anything "particular"?

Of course, what such speakers and writers were inveighing against was exclusivism. Well, already this isn't friendship. When you have committed yourself to community life and you enter into so exclusive a relationship with one other person or other persons that you simply close all the remaining people out of your life, this is not friendship. It is not only a matter of what you are doing to the other potential friends, what you are not allowing to develop in them because you are not giving your attention to them; but even in relation to this one person, you do not have friendship but merely a mutual devouring process. I am so busy devouring you and letting you devour me that we haven't time for anyone else even to nibble at us or find out what we are like. So, this was what was meant; but I would say it was a very unfortunate way of expressing it. I think we should just declare that we do not want exclusiveness, neither in religious life nor in society. You couldn't have this even in marriage. If a woman was so taken up with her husband that she couldn't bother to take care of their children, this would be a very peculiar kind of wife.

Then, on the very darkest level, this "particular friendship" alluded to meant a perverted love, a sexually perverted love. You feel a love for one of your own sex that would be the normal love of a woman's heart for a man, for a husband. Well, these things can happen. We should realize that they are perversions; they are not run-of-the-mill material. We do not want to cast down our eyelashes and think that we are nuns and don't ever have to advert to the darker things of life. That's nonsense. But neither do we need to establish a workshop about this because such things are just too rare. We know that they can happen, that it is something to be concerned about, but not something to have a seminar about. Possibility is not synonymous with actuality, much less with epidemic.

What we want to have in a community is a particular friendship, in the only true meaning the term can have, with every sister in that community. Well, what am I handing to you now? Am I presenting you with some impossible theory that you can feel just the same toward each sister in the community? Of course not. I just said it was *particular*. So, it has got to be different with every sister. And this, too, is where I think religious get into a lot of troublous thinking, and especially young religious—even mature religious like *you*! I mean, thinking that you have to feel the same for every person, about every person. Nonsense. We must not confuse the degree of intimacy with friendship per se. There is no reason in a religious community why each sister should not have a friendship with every other sister. In fact, it is wrong if she hasn't. But we must work to establish this, and I mean *work*, because respect—looking again and again—is work. It is much less challenging, it is much lazier, just to take one look and say, "No, not my type." Then we are finished with the relationship with this person, except on the normal civil level that we have to maintain in any sort of social life.

So, it's work to establish friendship with people. As I mentioned before, it takes patience to understand. And we know that patience can be the hardest work in all the world. But now, about feeling the same toward everyone: you can never aspire to have the same degree of intimacy with every person in the community. This is ridiculous, because this kind of relationship is established by affinities. And we cannot manufacture affinities. We cannot manufacture the same tastes and reactions, and it would be just too gruesome if we did. Imagine, if we all had only one thought on a subject, if we had only one reaction to each situation. Life would be so dreary it would be impossible. This is what I mean, about devouring one another's potential. We want to recognize the differences in one another, not with sorrow or disappointment, but in order to esteem and respect them. We want to come to have real reverence for this person who is so different from me.

2

"... As I Have Loved You": Loving Others into Lovableness

You know the famous quotation from Blessed Giles of Assisi, the one I have spoken about and written about: that the greatest gift a person can have under heaven is to know how to live well with those with whom he dwells. Simple little statement! but it shows what a profound theologian Blessed Giles was. The grace to live well with those with whom he dwells.... Let us reflect on that.

How do we live well? To live well means to live fully, and that goes back again to helping the other person become the person God meant her to be and that she cannot be without the help of other people. So that is the point. If you live alone, you can build up a whole fantasy about yourself because you've never had the occasion to let other people help you discover who you are. And we all know that there are many times when they seem to be entirely too helpful! We are not always ready to recognize some of these things.

How much do we learn about ourselves from our reactions to other people! How many infelicitous reactions do we discover, things we'd much rather not know about ourselves! The little flares of irritability come up in us, the

annoyances at other people's reactions to things, the whole
dreary litany of other like things that you just might possibly know. But when we find out by this action and interaction with others what we are really like and what our
own weaknesses are, we also learn what our strength is. We
likewise discover in ourselves some beautiful reactions of
compassion and understanding—sometimes even of
patience—and we cannot discover these things alone.

You know the homely little tale often told about the hermit, the very holy hermit who had lived in the desert for
years and years. He had no possessions, he fasted strictly,
and he had come to think, as I suppose one could easily be
tempted to think if left to one's own unaided speculations,
that he was a fair sort of fellow in God's eyes. But in his
naiveté he brought this to God's attention. You remember
how he reminded God that he was so detached from everything, how he was really living his life completely for God—
and a few other points for God's edification. And the Lord
informed the self-complacent hermit that he was more
attached to the cat he had than the king of France was
attached to all his possessions. It is my personal conclusion
that the holy hermit must have been pretty well shaken by
this divine observation.

Since we are not living as hermits, we have a lot of inter-
mediaries to bring things to our attention. God doesn't have
to appear and tell us, "Look, you're not cutting nearly so
good a figure in my eyes as you seem to think you are."
Also, there is a very heartening other side to that coin. Sometimes we may be cutting a far better figure in God's eyes
than we think we are. And community life helps us to attain
the consolation of realizing this side, too. There are our
clearer-eyed moments when we are willing to admit that
we were at fault in a situation, when we see our sisters so

patient with us. How much we can be moved by this compassion and this patience of other people! Have you never arrived at the heady conclusion, after realizing your great fault in a situation or a series of situations, and experienced the exuberance of the discovery, Look at what I am! This is how they see me. This is what I have done. And they still let me stay here! They still put up with me; they still even smile at me; they still act as if they don't mind having me around, but even seem to enjoy it. Well, dear sisters, if you have never experienced that, I hope that you soon will, because this is a wonderful discovery.

When we see our sisters react like this, we do receive light on our own faults. We cannot, however, take too much of this light at one time. "I have many things to tell you, but you cannot bear them now" (Jn 16:12). But as we become able to tolerate more such light, we also come to the realization of how much these other people who see our shoddiness, our loose edges, our sagginess, our dreariness day after day, love us. So we touch down on humility. And that is such a happy landing strip. It usually takes us much longer to see ourselves than it takes our sisters to see us; and, of course, this works for everyone. These other people who are around at my worst moments, because they are always around, do still love me. They do still want me. They are still interested in me. Well, this certainly gives us a new insight into God's love for us. If my sisters who are finite can still love me when they know me so well, then what about the infinite God? They can love me only finitely, and they do. He can love me infinitely, and he does. So there are two sides to the coin of letting other people reveal us to ourselves. It isn't only a matter of seeing our deficiencies but of seeing how much we are still loved in spite of our deficiencies and maybe even because of them.

Now the last thread of these thought-skeins I want to throw out before we go into more detail on them is this realization of our potential. I touched on it at the beginning. If we do not love each sister with a love of friendship, in that same degree we are hindering her from being what God wants her to be. That is a large thought, and I want you to do some large thinking about it. It is too lazy an approach merely to examine a thought like this which is true, which is theologically valid, which is psychologically firm. You can admit it, affirm it, advert to it in passing, and then put it away, never making it practical, never working it into the fabric of your own daily lives.

We say that some people are lovable, but these are the people whom we have allowed to be lovable. The love of friendship even changes the loved one's physical appearance in our eyes. For example, I remember bringing home a class picture when I was, I think, a sophomore in high school, and my mother commenting that a certain girl was "sweet, but so plain". I just couldn't take this in, because I loved this person so much. My mother knew that I did, and she was merely remarking that the girl was so much plainer than her sister. But I really had to think about this for a long while, because I'd always thought my mother had very good judgment and here she was making a perfectly ridiculous remark! For this girl was beautiful. It was obvious to me that this girl was beautiful. It took me some time to realize that my mother was looking at a face, and I was looking at a person whom I loved. And she was physically beautiful to me because I loved her. It wasn't that I loved this person despite the fact that she wasn't pleasant to look at; it was that I loved her so much that I thought she was very pleasant to look at. It is love that educates our judgments.

Now, if we can do this even with physical features, we can do it with psychological features, too. If we stop at the psychological minor facts about the other person, at the psychological moles and the emotional warts, then, yes, we will say, what a pity this person is so plain, so ugly, so homely. But it is your love that will make her beautiful. Your love that will make her lovable. And the only way that people can become lovable is by our loving them. After all, this is the only claim that we have for being lovable. God has first loved us, and that is why we are lovable. We are beautiful because he loves us. Just cogitate on that again, please! We are beautiful in God's sight because he loves us; we are lovable in his sight because he loves us. And this is the solitary claim to lovableness that we have.

This certainly works on the human plane as well. What did our Lord mean when he said, "Love one another as I have loved you" (Jn 13:34)? I *made* you lovable by loving you. If we had no book, then, no tape recorder, nothing else to meditate on for the rest of our lives, except "love one another as I have loved you", we wouldn't ever run out of material. And even on our deathbed we would have to tell God to wait—we haven't finished our meditation.

If we were really to think profoundly about this, dear sisters, we would wake up. We are supposed to act toward one another as God acts. We are not asked to be humanly great as the world judges greatness. No, we are just asked to be like God! It isn't that we are merely asked to overcome our faults, but that we are invited to "be perfect as your heavenly Father is perfect" (Mt 5:48). This is the kind of thought that God gives us. It leaves us reeling, but still it is the kind of thought that liberates us. It teaches us how to pray, how to be contemplatives. If you take this thought, these words that our Lord gave to us, you don't need much else. This is why, in the history of monasticism, we notice that the greatest contemplatives didn't need much else. They beheld the Word of truth.

Now you understand that I do not mean to belittle the place of the library. In fact, you well know how much importance I attach to it, to books, to tapes, all the rest. But I am saying that we already have this in essence. All the books that have ever been written on the spiritual life are simply trying to tell us something about what God has already told us in the Scriptures. As I've said before, what he said is so devastatingly simple that we need five hundred books to help us come, in our little complicated way, to understand what our Lord meant when he said, "Love one another as I have loved you." What he meant when he said, "By this [and by nothing else!] will all men know that you are my followers, that you love one another" (Jn 13:35). So we are very indebted to the kind persons who write hundreds and hundreds of books so that we can come in our limping, complex way into some glimmer of the great dazzling light of our Lord's simple words.

It would be a terrible thing, wouldn't it, if we in the cloister, who live the closest kind of community life in the Church, in society, were not helping one another to be lovable? You know from your own experience how you react when you feel that someone doesn't like you. If you have had this experience in the world (and who hasn't!), or even in religious life, that someone is registering disapproval of you, you tend to turn right in upon yourself or aggressively out upon the other. According to what type of personality you are, you will express your reaction in one way or another. Maybe you will pull your real self out of sight, like a turtle pulling its head in under its shell. And you will stay right there, instead of growing from this experience and out of it. To change our figure of speech, what would happen to a bud if, instead of putting out its petals as it matured, it got to be a tighter and tighter bud? You can't do that. A bud persisting in remaining a bud is doomed to die. It will wither and droop on the stem. You simply cannot stay a bud forever; you have got to put out your petals. Or, if you are a different type of personality you may become aggressive when you grow aware that someone does not seem to like you. Whose fault is this? Partly yours and partly the other person's.

You are never completely yourself unless you know yourself to be loved. I've said that before, and I shall say it again, because I attach very great importance to it. No one, and especially not a woman, can be fully herself except when she is loved.

I know a very touching story about the late Father Daniel Lord. I must have told some of you, for it moves me very much. Do any of you know him? Oh, he's too old, hmm? Well, he was not a very good writer. His books do not provide the best way to get to know him. He knew that he was a mediocre writer. He said, "I am not a literary man." But he was something much more important—a very wonderful person. I knew him fairly well. I worked with him, I was in some of his plays. This man, this holy Jesuit priest, was a most outgoing type of person. He was the never-knew-a-stranger type and always the center of action. Always where the action was, he more especially created the action. He *was* the action. And I think this man would have given anyone the impression that he was completely "established" socially.

Father Lord had a million friends. Youth ran after him like a pied piper. You would suppose this priest had no security problem. He was at home everywhere. But when he died, a very good friend of his let me know what Father

Daniel Lord had confided to him. If Father came into a room and knew there was just one person there who didn't like him, then he could not be completely himself. And his friend said that Father Lord suffered keenly from knowing he was disliked by many people. Well, I knew that he was disliked by some. Any outstanding person is bound to be disliked by small persons. Our Holy Father Francis said, "Pull down the cedars and maybe the little underbrush will show." But that such an immensely gifted man suffered so much from dislike is, I think, a classic example of the fact that no one is free from this. It is only that we see it more readily in the more reserved person, the more timid person. But it is perfectly normal to want to be loved. And everyone suffers from a lack of being loved. If we say to ourselves, I live for God! (which I do, of course) and I don't care what people think of me, it doesn't matter a bit to me—then we are liars, dear sisters, and the truth is not in us. Everyone loves to be loved.

It is sometimes said that we should not just tolerate one another, but really accept one another. That is not the way I would prefer you to think about "tolerate". This is a word, in company with other words, that has suffered so much from false connotations. It is a very beautiful word. "Tolerate" comes from the Latin *tollere*, which is "to carry" or "to bear up" or "to bear the weight of". And we have come to use the word in a very supine sense. By saying that we tolerate people, we usually mean that we "put up with" people. And what really underlies that is something very patronizing, something very condescending. I, from my great height, will put up with this creature who is on a lower level. With the sweep of my vision I will try to overlook all the deficiencies in her. This is a frightful distortion of a very beautiful word, but I'm afraid that is the way the word is most often used. We say to a person, "Why aren't you more tolerant?" meaning, "Why don't you 'put up with' others better than you do?"

When we really look into the meaning of the word, I think we get a lot of food for meditation. For if we are really tolerating our sisters, then we should already be very well equipped for friendship with them. If we are truly tolerating them, we are really carrying them along, we are bearing them up, we are shouldering them in a sense and swinging them along. So, to tolerate one another is precisely what we should do, but not in the sense in which this is often unhappily understood.

We were talking about being accepted and how our attitude toward persons effects a change in that person. That is, it effects something that might not be visible to other people who do not love and understand that person. I have given you the little example of my friend, the girl whom I could not imagine another would not think beautiful, because I loved her so much that, of course, she had become beautiful to me. Now let's look at that from the other angle. If it is only when we love one another, really are friends with one another, that the true image of each of us can emerge, well, this already explains why there are so many caricatures in life, so many masks, so many false images.

You know, when I have to leave our enclosure and travel around the country on my visitations of our other monasteries, and I see what many women "outside" look like, what many people of both sexes look like, what their expressions are, I am struck so much by this sense of caricature. Too many women aren't feminine anymore. They don't look like beautiful women anymore; they look freakish. I think there is something more here than just the case of a cloistered nun obliged to wander on occasion out into "the world"

who discovers new fashions and wrings her hands, thinking
how strange people look. No, it isn't that at all. I am interested in new things. I don't expect people to wear the fashions they wore when I entered the cloister or the fashions
they wore last year, for that matter. But this is something
else.

It is not that people have changed "à la mode", you might
say—just changed the style. No, there's something deeply
wrong here. Why are men looking effeminate, and why
have some women lost their femininity? What is underly-
ing all this? Why are people afraid to look like themselves?
Why all this false hair, tiers of eyelashes, and this clownish
paint which is no longer what I think makeup was meant
to be—something to enhance what is already there. Why
has this travesty on makeup become instead something to
distort, something which repels? Why are some women not
willing to be feminine anymore? Why are some men willing to look effeminate? Well, I think this goes deeply into
the meaning of caricature.

This is what we can do, too, in a certain way, in a psychological sense. We haven't much area to do this, in the line of
clothes, admittedly. Still less with makeup, which we don't
have at all. But we can do it in an even worse way. We can
retreat from the image of ourselves that we either have never
fully discovered because of not being loved enough or which
we are unwilling to recognize as our own image because it
has been repudiated by others. I think that is rather important, that duality. We become unwilling to present our own
image either because we do not recognize it because it has
not been lovingly recognized by others; or, recognizing it,
we deny it because it has been rejected by others.

Now, you know what a caricature is. It is usually effected
by distorting a person's image through bringing out one

feature at the expense of others. Caricature is sometimes amusing, sometimes cruel. But there is another meaning of caricature. This is the ludicrously poor imitation. And this is what we can do psychologically to ourselves and to others. We can present a ridiculously poor imitation of ourselves for one of the two reasons we just considered. Now, this is a big burden for us to take on, especially in community where we live so closely. Are we perhaps contributing to the creation of caricatures of our sisters? You know, we see this all the time. Not only in unfeminine styles, the false hair, the freakish modes and so on; but you see it in habits of behavior in people who are unwilling or afraid to face what they truly are.

Why do we see young girls trying to dress and act like fully grown women, and on the other end see aging women trying desperately to look and act like young girls? We see that it is all upside down and each one becoming a caricature of herself because she is unwilling to be the person she really is and that she actually is at this time. These things appear externally, but there are patterns of behavior that are not so obvious but which are really rooted in this same thing. You find people who are afraid, afraid not to be loved. These persons will become very cold and withdrawn. You hear about icy personalities. Often it is not a basic truth at all. This may be a very warm, affectionate person who is so afraid of not being accepted as herself that she has been lured into this sense of aloofness from people. She tells herself that it doesn't matter if they accept her or not. If she chooses to be withdrawn and aloof, then she doesn't run the risk of giving out her warmth and her love and possibly having it rejected.

You see how people who feel inferior do this sometimes. The people who suffer the most from inferiority complexes are often the most swaggering. Bold people are frequently those who feel second-rated, people who have not yet reached the bully stage but who are already arrogant. These are so often persons who are actually very unsure of themselves. Those who do not suffer from a sense of inferiority don't have the driving need to establish themselves. They can relax. Let's see now; I have jotted down several examples: youth putting on age, age putting on youth, inferiority putting on swagger, fear putting on coldness. And all these things come from a lack of self-esteem, a lack of sureness about myself. Usually, almost always, this lack of self-esteem has been encouraged by others.

3

The Path to Peace:
Action, Reaction, and Interaction

We have spent quite a bit of time in examining the things we discover about ourselves in living closely with other people. We've seen a number of dreary things about ourselves, but also a number of good things. If our sisters did not have faults, we would not have any functional area for compassion. We might not even discern this well of compassion in ourselves. But the fact remains that in our plumbings, we have also found a number of things that are not too pleasant to behold. We can discover depths of compassion but also depths of severity, harshness, coldness. We find all the possibilities of virtue and vice. And insofar as we don't live in friendship with other people, we don't discover any of these things. For they are not found on a superficial plane and seldom hit upon by loners.

Why are we going around and around in world affairs right now, trying to find peace? Well, I suppose I could be accused of vast oversimplification if I said that it is because people aren't friends with one another. Yet, if we reduce the present world situation to its basics, what must we conclude? And if we stop and reduce certain situations

in religious communities at present to their basics, what
will be our findings? I think we shall see that it is idiotic
not to be friends with one another, and this idiocy is bed-
rock to world problems and community problems.

Look, dear sisters, what do we have? The psalms say, seventy years "or eighty if we are strong". That isn't much
time. When you were fifteen, it may have seemed like quite
a bit of time; but now that you are in your twenties, it
doesn't seem quite so long, does it? And when you catch
up with me and realize that you're already more than half-
way there, it will not seem very long at all. So, we have
seventy or eighty years. And we are put on earth together.
For us, there is the specific additional "together" of an
enclosed community life as contemplative nuns. And we all
hope to enjoy eternal happiness in the vision of God with
one another. Shall we then spend these seventy or eighty
years making life miserable for one another and, most especially, for ourselves?

Now, I said that it might seem a facile oversimplification
to say that if people were friends we would not have any
wars, that if nations were friends we would not need to
have these sometimes grotesque round-table talks on peace
that are often parodies on peace. But, you know, in that
oversimplification there is this one good element: it's true.

It is surprising, isn't it, what history shows us can be
done if we work with elemental truth. Look at what our
Father Saint Francis did. This one undersized man with
this big idea that you should simply preach the good news
that people ought to love one another and that when you
greet them you shouldn't have a chip on your shoulder but
should say, "Peace and blessing! May the Lord give you his
peace, my friend." Yes, look what he did! If I remember
correctly, this one little man changed the course of history

in Europe in his time. He turned the whole medieval society upside down, didn't he?—and with this "vast oversimplification"! I think Francis accomplished quite a bit more than the learned men who said, "Now these issues are very complicated; we must study them at length"—which is sometimes another way of saying that we'll just fight about this until we die. And so we do not want to label and dismiss simplification too lightly. This is the truth. As I have often told you about simplicity, unadorned truth is usually a little more than we can take. Simplicity is so overpowering that we like to retreat into complexity and say, this is nonsense, that you can solve all the world's problems with friendship. But actually, this is the only way they will ever be solved. And what we attain at the kind of meetings often held, sincerely intended as they may be, are merely painful truces that may at best establish a little interim until the next war breaks out. It is only friendship that will reestablish what Christ came to establish.

So, what does all this have to do with community life? Well, everything, I think. Because the friendship in which we should excel will somehow affect the world. This is our contribution to world peace, this friendship that we have right here, what we are doing for one another, how we are helping one another to develop.

Now there are some things I just touched on last time and that I said we would go into later. Well, now it's later! There was that idea of affection and that nagging question—How can I "be friends with everyone", when I know that I don't feel the same toward everyone, even that I *can't* feel the same toward everyone. But part of this seeming problem (it is only seeming, you know) is that we do not differentiate between intuition and developing understanding. We surely have all had this experience on occasion of meeting persons whom we have immediately loved. This is intuitive friendship. There is no one here who has never had this experience, is there? Good.

One outstanding example of this in my own life is my first meeting with Dr. Andrée Emery. Among hundreds of religious superiors at that one meeting the contemplatives were summoned to attend, I had many very pleasant encounters; but with this great woman, there was something different: an immediate intuition of friendship. Now, you obviously feel this for some persons and you do not feel it for others. And I think that sometimes we make a major mistake in the area of conceptual friendship because of this. Intuitive friendship is a great blessing, and also a very rare one. We must not get the false idea that we have no basis for friendship with those for whom we do not feel this immediate intuitive affection.

Real friendship is a developing, evolving affair. Even a friendship begun with this intuitive affection has to develop. If it doesn't, it will sputter out. And sometimes intuitions do not develop. Sometimes the intuition may even be proved false. And other times the loss of the intuitive *feeling* of affection is no reason at all for not awaiting the development of a very good friendship with this person, growing out of richer soil than mere intuition that may prove to be the root of a perennial or may not.

I said last time that we have to be patient with friendship. There is instant coffee and instant tea, but there is no such thing as instant understanding. Understanding, more often than not, involves a very slow process. The longer we know one another, the longer we are friends with one another, the better do we come to understand one another. Dear sisters, I want you to get this very straight in your minds: nobody is ever going to be perfectly understood. There have been old songs and old jeremiads from time immemorial that "nobody understands me". This is very true. Nobody understands me perfectly and nobody on earth understands any one of you perfectly, except God. For to understand a person perfectly you have, in a sense, to *be* that person—or to have created that person. You see that this is rather obviously restricted to God! However, we do grow in understanding, and we have to allow for slow growth.

Remember how I counselled against lowering your head and charging into one another in a kind of bulldog determination to understand one another? I think this is sometimes the particular hazard for young people. They want very much to understand one another, to be helpful toward one another. In a misguided effort to achieve excellent goals, they try to break through doors and windows in other people. You can't do this. What you can do is to stay around and wait until the person herself opens a door or a window. See—don't break it, but wait until she opens it. And then, be there, be there to understand her.

And how do you learn to discipline yourself for this waiting? Well, certainly you are right that we have to be driven by a holy discontent; but we cannot be cruel—even to ourselves. We cannot try to act with ourselves as if original sin had never happened, as though we had never weakened ourselves by our own accumulation of faults. There is no surer way to strangle charity, to abort charity in the spiritual or psychological womb if you want to put it that way, than to be too severe with ourselves. So much is cautioned against being too easy with ourselves, and that is certainly an attitude we don't want to espouse. But there is also danger in being too severe, and it is difficult to get a balance here.

You don't want to go to the other extreme and just say, "Well, you know, I'm only human", when you have been short, impatient, unwilling to try to understand. When has humanity, which I grant is a fact, been an excuse against heroism? Usually this kind of thing goes by temperament. Most phlegmatic persons are inclined to say, "I'm only human. What do you expect? I'm doing my best." And the choleric person wants to take herself by the throat and strangle herself when she doesn't think she is making any progress. Both are wrong, of course. You don't want to strangle yourself, but you can give yourself a good spiritual swat once in a while. You don't want to whimper, "I'm only human", but to prod yourself on. And yet, you are content to learn from your mistakes. If we commit a fault, if we see a deficiency in charity and learn from it, then I think we are growing in charity by patience with ourselves, which can be very demanding. It takes a lot of maturity to be both firm and patient with ourselves.

Frustrating lack of success after all your efforts? Well, our Lord never asked us to succeed—lucky us!—he just asked us to keep trying. What about his college of apostles? Look what a consolation they are! Certainly they were meant to be a kind of friendship-seminar incarnate, just as we in our cloister are. And certainly no one ever had a better Person to teach them, to direct discussions, than the apostles had. They had God right there. Yet how unwilling they sometimes were to admit their mistakes, to face reality, to be the real persons they were. They dropped back and were having a good old free-for-all as to who was going to be the head of this assembly. Remember that place in Scripture? And our Lord said (Oh, how I love this part!), "'What were you speaking about?' And they held their peace" (Mk 9:33–34). You can just bet they did! And these were the persons who became martyrs, who became perfected in charity, which is what it is to be a martyr. And they had to learn slowly, even under such tutelage. Look at them at the very Ascension of the Lord. What was their last word to him before our Lord took off into the clouds? "Is this the time that you will establish the kingdom in Israel" (Acts 1:6)? Can you imagine anything more "frustrating", dear sisters, for our Lord? After his Resurrection and even on the Mount of the Ascension, his apostles and disciples still thought their own plans might be going to come off. They were still missing the point, and rather completely. But our Lord did not say, "What's the use?" He ascended into heaven. Is that not a salutary morsel for our reflection?

Another important aspect involved here is that we don't suddenly make major choices about our personality—it has, on the contrary, been prepared for by many minor choices. We do not suddenly say to ourselves, "I am not an acceptable person. Look how they act when I say what I really think." And so on, and so on. "So, I quit. I am going to lock the door and decide to be somebody else." No, we don't do that, of course; but we do something much worse, really. Because that kind of monologal hyperbole can be easily turned off. You can see one major wrong decision, and you can undo it. But there are the little choices, small continuing choices that gnaw away at ourselves. The results of erosion are much harder to repair than a clean break is to mend.

What are you supposed to do about adverse reactions? Always try to look for what it is in you or your manner or your tone or whatever that may have elicited a reaction that hurts you. You can learn immensely much from this. And if you can determine to grow in maturity on the occasions when you may be even deeply hurt but force yourself to say, "What in me made her react like that?"

then you have found a way to learn about yourself, which amounts to a crash course (in the best sense of the term) and which, in the end, is most rewarding.

Even if the other person is really wrong, even if her reaction really has not been charitable, has not been what it should be, you can still learn so much. This is more a duality than an ambivalence: I am not accepted—but how did I present myself? And this goes back and forth, and back and forth—this is the way we learn. No, it is not right that someone seems to reject me. But what was perhaps not right in my presentation that provoked this rejection? If we can gradually establish ourselves on that level of womanly self-questioning (and I underscore *gradually* because we are so foolish if we think we can take one mighty leap and arrive at maturity), we are increasingly better equipped for friendship with God and with our sisters. The reaction of fallen human nature when someone reacts toward us in a way that is unpleasant or unfair is most often the "poor me" attitude. "I'm only trying to be good, and they don't understand me, and so what's the use." And then we are right back to where we started: nobody understands me.

How do you go about achieving this objective look at yourself and your manner without getting emotionally sucked under? Well, that's a good question. The genuine sixty-four-dollar question. You have to face the fact that it *is* difficult. Anyone can do what's easy. We all get so blinded by emotions sometimes; and the more we are emotionally aroused out of bounds, the less clearly we can think on any issue. Now, I wouldn't be human if I weren't hurt or maybe "hot" when I feel my opinions are being rejected, when someone looks displeased at what I've said or someone flashes me a look that indicates rather clearly that she thinks I spoke in the wrong way or that I spoke out of turn. It's very, very difficult not to get lost in an emotional fog then. And as I said, we react according to what type personality we are. Maybe we close in on ourselves so that we won't get hurt like that again. "I'll show them. I just won't say what I think about anything anymore. I'll just let *them* talk." Or maybe again, being of a more aggressive psychological complexion, we get indignant to the point that we may be even semihostile toward everybody in general. "What's the use! You can't say anything! Free speech! Ha—just let me say something, and see what happens!"

A natural (as distinguished from supernatural) reaction usually runs along one of those tracks or any of the other paths that fallen human nature will take when someone has touched a nerve in us. But such tracks and such paths will detour us from really knowing ourselves and helping us to present to others the real person that they just didn't see—perhaps because our presentation didn't allow them to see. After all, we wouldn't really set out to be repulsive! I think this is more a natural "talent" we all share on occasion than something we need to strive after. No one deliberately drops a statement just to annoy someone else. And so we ask, "Well, why didn't I come across in what I said?" Was it the manner, the tone, the expression? What was it?

Another question: Do we *have* to be emotionally involved at all? The answer is yes, of course. God equipped us with an emotional apparatus, and it's very good equipment to have. We must never set false goals for ourselves. When we come out with our bright idea and others are less than dazzled we can't try to fool ourselves that we don't care at all, that we are not emotionally involved, that we should just say, "I'm so detached, I'll offer it all up for missionaries." This is artificial. If we are honest (and we've got only honest people here!) we do want to be accepted, we do like to have our ideas approved. And here's another thing: we need both approval and the revelation of our shortcomings.

This is important: approval is necessary in order to be able to bear disapproval. It is all too easy, emotionally involved as we are (and remember, if we were not attached to our opinions they would not be our opinions), to turn away disapproval without looking for what is good for us in it. We were reflecting at the beginning of these talks on friendship about our responsibility toward one another, but we also have a responsibility toward ourselves to see into and learn from situations. We can be only too easily tempted to declare that the person who brings some of our shortcomings to our attention or the person who may seem to thwart us or seem to disapprove of us is wrong. We insist that she is wrong because we are so afraid that she may be at least partly right. I really don't think there's any adverse reaction we can ever get from which we cannot draw some little grain of self-knowledge and, hopefully, self-improvement.

Maybe we discover a great lack of tact in ourselves. And tact, in my opinion, is one of the greatest natural virtues. Never play down tact as though it were for sissies, whereas *we* are frank, honest people who lay it right on the line. Nobody can afford to have everything laid right on the line. Tact is a strong womanly virtue, not a "girlish" virtue. Our dear Lord was extremely tactful.

We can, of course, get lost in the wrong kind of introspection as well as "ultraspection". We do not want to investigate one another's privacy, but we want to understand one another as much as we are allowed. And we want to understand ourselves, as best we can, without disassembling the parts for study and research. That kind of thing is apt to leave us with one spring left over when we have reassembled the parts. But we want to face ourselves as well as to rejoice in what may just happen to be right in ourselves. Some modern psychologists exaggerate our conditioning by the past. Certainly we are all conditioned by our past, but we cannot blame our present behavior entirely on our past. That is just an alibi. Conditioned by it, yes; but we can't hide behind it. The mere fact that we recognize conditioning factors in our past life already indicates that we have the ability to cope with them and not hide behind them. Get out in front of them and look at them. Let us never inflate unhappy experiences of the past. There is no one who has not had some sorrowful experience, and some have had many and in a marked degree. But from the same sorrowful or even harrowing experiences, one person will emerge integral and the other will be harmed.

God first loved us, we have reflected, and this made us lovable. But action and result cannot be separated except in sentence structure. They are interknit, woven together into the fabric of living, into the stuff of our humanity. Of course we must love in order to discover the love in the other person, but at the same time she must love me in order to discover my lovableness. And this is acting and reacting and interacting all the time. For both of us it is the mystery of loving and being loved.

So this is what is so marvelous about friendship: it takes two persons to have this action and interaction. You don't have one person loving the other person and understanding her, but you have two persons accepting each other, loving each other, and growing in affection for each other, in mature affection that accepts elements that do not evoke affection. If we try to build a community of friendships, this is always going to be a happy place, this religious community of ours, to live in.

4

Genuine Friendship in a Seedbed of Honesty

Recently I came across an intriguing little book by Father Ignace Lepp, *The Ways of Friendship*.[1] Some of you are familiar, I'm sure, with this well-known priest-psychiatrist. Now, there is nothing quite so satisfying as finding that a professional person proven worthy of great esteem is saying exactly the same thing you have said yourself! You want to comment, "What a bright fellow this is!" We were discussing in an earlier conference the irrectitude of tagging either an exclusivist attachment or a perverted attraction with the title "particular friendship" and concluded that a genuine friendship cannot possibly be anything else but particular, whereas the types of relationships that frequently are dubbed with this term do not qualify as friendships at all. Well, here is Father Ignace Lepp, saying on page twenty-two, "As though friendship could be anything but particular!"[2] As I say, one gets this happy feeling welling up within that here we have a manifestly intelligent man making an obviously insightful observation because it is what we have ourselves observed!

[1] Ignace Lepp, *The Ways of Friendship* (New York: Macmillan, 1966).
[2] Ibid., p. 22.

47

But seriously, now, dear sisters, we do want to return to this idea and examine it from yet another angle. For I believe there is an especially marked tendency right now in some areas to swing to an opposite extreme from mistakes of the past. It is a fact that formerly there was a tendency in some communities to disfavor warm friendships among the sisters. As our Mother Immaculata[3] cryptically used to remark, "Too much was said about particular friendships and too little about particular enmities."

Somehow, in certain places, a false ideal was held before young religious: that the spiritual life is exclusively an affair of "God and I". Now, we could develop this thought into a valid and meaningful theology of personal holiness. But I am afraid that the way it was all too often understood, even if this was not intended, was that it is "God and I" in the sense that other people are simply present for the practical purposes of living and have no personal connection with me and my holiness. Other people are just ... here. We live in the same house and supposedly have the same goal; but I live my life, and ... well, please don't bother me. And, of course, there is point number two in this outline for holiness, which is: you live your life; it has nothing in particular to do with mine. The conclusion was that the more I am concerned with God and with nobody else, the holier I am. This is a heinous fallacy and falsity, even heresy, sisters. "Love one another as I have loved you", Christ said (Jn 15:12). And his love was not—is not—an aloof, disinterested, "detached" love. Now, however, instead of correcting that aberration, we sometimes seem to be going over to the other extreme so that there is a tendency in many

---

[3] Foundress of the Roswell Monastery of Poor Clares, d. February 23, 1972.

places "to understand" people until we have emotionally and psychologically reduced them to a pulp, or to pry into them in the way that one opens a can with a can opener.

Each of us has a right to her privacy, and we shall want to remember this if the friendships we are interested in building are to be genuine friendships. This is where we want to establish our balance and sense of values. The professed nuns discussed this at some length when we took C. S. Lewis' *The Four Loves*[4] in our cultural reading program. The one of the four loves—that is, affection, friendship, charity, and eros—which Lewis considers the highest love is the love of friendship. There were a number of interesting insights expressed on this.

Some of you will remember the discussion when the novices came along and some were puzzled because they had had a constricted view of friendship. I discovered that some had the idea that all authentic friendship is expressed by the sharing of the deepest intimacies of thought and experience and opinions. Now, as I reminded you when we started this series, there are degrees of friendship. And there should be and must be in a religious community dedicated to a single goal and sharing a common dedication to essentials, friendship between and among all the members. But these friendships develop in varying degrees and on different planes. They cannot all be the same. And remember this, dear sisters: friendship is a matter of emotional energy, not of intellect.

When we see a person who seems very poor in friendship capacity, this does not inevitably indicate that that person is impoverished intellectually, but it does mean that she is impoverished emotionally. So, this is one of the

[4] C. S. Lewis, *The Four Loves* (London: Geoffrey Bles, 1960).

underdevelopments we help one another to correct. But friendship, in the sense of this deep intimacy of spirit and, above all, as concerns a deep intimacy of soul, is possible with only a very, very limited group of persons, perhaps with only one person. And this is where the confusion comes in.

I remember one professed sister asking me, "Well, how can this be in our way of life? Is this not something that belongs only to my relationship with my superior?" Well, I would say, maybe, yes, and maybe, no. That reminds me of a professor in forensics I had in days of yore. He answered all thorny questions with this reply: "Well, yes. And then again, no." After having said which, he always swallowed noticeably, cleared his throat impressively, and observed a half minute of silence before changing the subject. You do need to have this relationship with someone. Normally, I think that you would be more inclined to give an intimacy of soul to the one who is set to direct you, guide you and help you, than you would to a peer. And you'll recall how quickly Saint Thérèse of Lisieux had ruefully to conclude that "spiritual sharings" with a peer were not availing for spiritual growth in the cloister. But that's not to say there are not exceptions. It is a large subject, and we shall want to consider it by itself another time. What I'm occupied with right now is that you get out of your minds as a difficulty, that when I speak of friendship I mean this very, very deep sharing of spiritual things.

This is not only impossible with a large group of persons, but it is most undesirable. To share with a whole group of persons the deepest intimacies of one's soul is a thing that I believe any normal person would consider most repugnant. If, for instance, God has given me a particular grace, a special spiritual joy, it would not be normal that I should want to race around telling everybody about it. There are, aren't there, the secrets of the King? If you have suddenly or gradually received in prayer or through some other channel a light about your own spiritual life or about a problem you have had, it would simply be a matter of taste that you did not gallop around to each sister and say the equivalent of, "Guess what?" So, let us put this supposed difficulty aside as being not a real difficulty. Such crude wholesale sharings would be not only an offense against spiritual good taste but would show a lack of the true contemplative spirit. It is normal to be shy about sharing one's spiritual life. It is nothing but crude to be ready to discourse on it to all and sundry.

So, when we speak about friendship, especially friendship in a religious community, we are referring to it in its broader sense. Now Father Ignace Lepp begins his book on the ways of friendship[5] by talking about loneliness, the tremendous loneliness in modern society. He is not writing about religious life in particular, although he often brings it into his considerations, but about society in general. He maintains that because people are so lonely, they seek the herd mentality. Let me herewith announce that I agree with him. I'm sure he will be relieved to know that! But, seriously now, it is true, isn't it? Undeniably true. Many people have in fact not developed as persons and so cannot bear to be alone for fear of finding out what God has really created in themselves.

We just read something along these lines this morning in Vatican II's *Decree on the Missions*. You recall how the document talked of the seed that is planted and how it has to have the nourishment of all the elements. It needs the soil,

[5] See Lepp, *Friendship*, pp. 11–21.

it needs the dew, it needs—help. No very startling idea, but I think it is a very good approach to friendship, too. We need one another; man *is* a social being, as has been noted for some thousands of years but perhaps not assimilated as a working idea. This is the way God created man. Now, when God further intensifies this idea of human community to religious community, we have a concentration and not a modification of God's creative plan. There is the human community, the Christian community, the ecclesial community, the religious community, the family community. Let's take another dip now into religious community to see that there, more than elsewhere and not less than elsewhere, do we need one another.

Friendship, dear sisters, is based on reciprocity. We've touched on that already. You can never have two persons only one of whom is a friend to the other. If you have some relationship like that which masks itself as friendship, be sure that it is nothing but selfishness. One person uses another person. When the former has a difficulty, she rushes to the latter person, to whom she has invalidly given the name "friend". But the same former person is not equally available to the same latter person. Nor has she any regard for the other's condition at the time she "needs" her. It doesn't matter to her. She has a difficulty she wants to unload, an opinion she wishes to give, a view she has to put forth. The other person is simply a receptacle. This is surely no friendship at all; it is without the reciprocity essential to friendship in which I give and I receive.

Now, oddly enough, although it may seem at first consideration that it is easier to receive than to give, that is often not so. It can sometimes require more humility to receive than to give. There is often enough not the experienced reward in receiving that there is in giving. It takes a certain depth of spirituality even to realize that receiving *is* a kind of giving, when the admission of my own inadequacies lets me give others the opportunity to help me or to supply for me. It requires humility to receive with graciousness. If it is possible to be lazy enough to let others do all the giving in community, it is also possible to be proud enough to refuse others the opportunity for giving.

Related to this is the "work loner". You sometimes find in community, sisters who are prodigies of generosity in their own charges. A certain sister will do anything, will give everything to the charge that she is given; and she will really do it with a loving zest that goes beyond the mere desire for approval to the point of sacrifice. She will give up her free time to take care of her work area in community. She will never need correction about the way she functions in her own charge. Yet this same sister may be an abysmal failure at general undertakings. A supposedly generous sister can be quite peevish and niggardly in a community effort. Now, this type of person has not developed her potential for friendship. How well am I able to relate to others in communal undertakings? How well do I relate to my community working as a team? How much am I able to receive from others in our common efforts?

And this, in turn, relates to some types of "dialogue" by which are meant a group of people sitting around a table, with each one trying to push her opinion down the throats of the others. Maybe there is a tremendous energy of "giving"; certainly there is no receiving. At one of our first federation chapters, Bishop Floyd Begin came to the meeting. Federation was then, of course, a new concept to us, and the bishop was explaining the functional aspects of the concept. I recall his pointing out that a federation meeting did not mean a coming together of delegations from every monastery, each delegation with its own preconceived ideas that were, obviously, the best by reason of their being its own ideas, and each delegation out to sell its ideas to the others. The bishop also described the wrong way to return to the home monastery after a federation meeting, which would be either to announce triumphantly, "Well, we won!" or to do the equivalent of throwing one's hat on the peg and muttering, "Well, we lost." Any degree or shade of that would indicate that there had been no real sharing, but only a coming together of persons with preconceived ideas that they would in no way alter. The only gain I could possibly see coming from this sort of thing would be the financial aid we would contribute to the airlines.

The person of intelligently strong convictions is ready to have them modified, expanded, or changed according to the counterevidence presented. Any persons of opposite convictions are friends to be listened to, not enemies to be warded off. So, as at work, as at meetings, we identify ourselves and we enlarge our personal capacity for friendly giving and receiving according as we can be authentic members of a group effort and not just determined loners.

But there is another kind of foxhole protection against the genuine communication that is essential to friendship. And that is talk which is not only noncommunicative but is actually a defense against any real communication. In speaking of the "total emptiness" of many conversations of young people, Father Lepp comments with what I consider great acuity that *because* they are incapable of any real communication, such persons hasten to meet again as soon as possible.[6] You see, in this way we can avoid the communication of solitude. Father goes on to say, "The

[6] Ibid., p. 15.

majority of relationships between adults are no better, and it is quite frightening to listen to conversations between people at a dinner or cocktail party."[7] And from that depressing evaluation, Father Lepp moves into the true meaning of communication that is so especially important for us as enclosed nuns.

I believe that three or four of you asked me, at the beginning of these conferences, how we can really develop friendship and communication in a community given to silence and solitude. It's a good question, but not too difficult to answer. Obviously, we cannot be talking to one another all day. But, is that necessary? I have just alluded to talk as often being a barrier to any real communication. And Father Ignace Lepp has this to say, which is so pertinent for us: "The hermit in the desert can communicate with God *and* with all those dear to him by prayer and reflection, and he can communicate with all mankind *if* his capacity for love has attained such universal dimensions."[8] The loner in community is not of community. She does not communicate with anyone. And she may even be radically incapable of real friendship and real communication, in which case it would be a tragic thing indeed that she had ever been admitted to a cloistered community where the members should really be experts in communication—the deep communication that is not dependent on words even while knowing how to make use of words. To arrive at a point where we might think we do not need communication with others is a dark achievement indeed, dear sisters. If we would ever feel that we don't really need one another, then we would merely be people living together in a house.

[7] Ibid.
[8] Ibid., p. 13 (emphasis added).

So we find ourselves returning to the point we've made before. We discover ourselves only in relation to others. And as we discover ourselves, we learn better how to communicate. As we expand sufficiently to communicate widely and profoundly, we emerge from any inner ghettos of opinions we may have either consciously or half-deliberately built up and come out into the sunlight of receiving even as we give, and giving while we receive. It is in growing in that communication ability which is essential to friendship that we discover in ourselves depths of compassion and depths of severity. And we have to be willing to recognize both in order to be true to ourselves and to others, and, above all, to God and his creation of us, which we have disordered and perhaps even seriously marred but which is basically good and beautiful.

There is nothing so salvifically disillusional as living in community. Remember the adverb there: salvifically! It's a healing, healthy disillusionment. False illusions about ourselves are dispelled in no way so well as by living in community, and perhaps particularly in the intense form of community that is an enclosed community. We are forced, if we are at all honest (which you are!), to discover new things about ourselves each day. And not all of them are unpleasant by any means, either. We get some happy surprises about ourselves. Remember, we touched on that before? We discover a generosity in ourselves that could not have expressed itself if others were not there to be its beneficiaries. Or, when someone in the community is in some particular need, whether physical, emotional, or whatever, don't we discover generosity welling up in us to help our sister who is the loved vehicle for the goodness in ourselves?

On the other hand, we do get the very helpful but not always very pleasant revelations about ourselves. We find out how selfish we can be, how very intolerant we can tend to be, whereas if we were living alone, a contemplative living somewhere in an apartment, we could live a whole lifetime through without discovering how really intolerant we can be, how energetically impatient, how selfish. In our little alcove, we could build up a false illusion that we are great souls of prayer, persons fitted and attuned to solitude. Community, dear sisters, community life richly lived, does not allow for illusions. It is a seedbed of honesty by which alone one grows in spirituality.

5

True Benevolence:
Respecting God's Mysteries of Love

In our last conference on friendship, we reflected at some length on communication, in its various expressions and on its different levels. We considered that real openness of mind which is not only not incompatible with strong convictions but should be a distinctive mark of persons of firm convictions. Strong, clear thinkers are never persons with closed minds. Then we talked of "loners" in the community and discovered that they are really outside community and "in" it only by way of physical locatedness. And we concluded that a real community where there is genuine communication and not just verbal exchange is a seedbed of honesty where we discover in a unique manner what is good about ourselves and what is not so good.

Now, we need both the approval of our sisters and the revelation that they give us, usually unconsciously and simply by our dealings with them, of our own shortcomings. Remember that approval is necessary, dear sisters, in order to bear disapproval. We said that before, and I remind you often enough at chapter[1] that it is so important that a sister

[1] The monastic chapter is the formal weekly assembly of the professed nuns, intended for the ongoing spiritual renewal of the community.—ED.

feel approved in her community. Even the superior, who has the grace to correct, will certainly effect no good in a person by saying the equivalent of, "Dear Sister, there is nothing right about you; everything is wrong. You might have some good qualities, but so far they have escaped me." You know that nobody is going to feel buoyed up by that to make a great new surge toward sanctity. But it is not only the superior who can paralyze a sister in this way. Our companions also could give us the impression that there really isn't much to us. And this could not help affecting the healthy self-esteem that we need, that ego strength of which I have spoken to you before.

Never allow yourself to build up this false illusion that you don't need other people. I warned you that this could be a particular hazard for the youngest religious in the community because it can be made to seem like an authentic spiritual goal: that the more I live with this "God and I" relationship, then the more perfect I am, the more holy I am. I called it a heresy, but sometimes it does not deserve so striking a tag. It is often enough mere triviality and sheer superficiality.

What do we mean when we say "God and I"? God is the Creator of all, Lover of all, the seat of all benevolence. That is a beautiful word, benevolence. You can see that the Latin root is clearly exposed in it: *bene* and *volo*, I wish well. God wishes well to all; and, therefore, if I am going to enter into a true God-and-I relationship, I must immediately accept the responsibility for all that are God's. If no one else really matters to me, if I am detached from everyone, it can be a case of my simply never having thought through what I am saying, that I am merely mouthing a word pattern whose profundity I have never perceived. The true understanding of God-and-I reveals to me that I enter into the interests of God, of the love of God, which is universal. And this is at the very heart of the contemplative life. I assume responsibility for everybody else in the world. As the Scriptures tell us, this is first expressed to those of my own household.

Our dear Father Treinen[2] said to me, in those few moments I had with him in the parlor before you came rattling in with your benches and guitars, that he had been working with some sisters of the active apostolate on their Constitutions in which they had this phrase: "Let us show love to all, but most especially to those who are in our employ." Now, they were evidently trying to correct a wrong from the past; but Father Treinen said to the committee head, "Good God, woman!—you've got the 'especially' in the wrong place. We must show love to all, especially to those of our own community." He said that if this is so, it will radiate out. And he is so right. If you have an intense love for the sisters of your own community, you are not going to be harsh toward the people you employ. If I really love you, I am not going to descend on the plumber like a virago. I have reminded you dozens of times that we are to the world, we are to the Church exactly what we are to one another, no more and no less. And if there is no real charity, no true bond of friendship and love in the community, there is no community. So, what is there to contribute to the community of the Church, to the community of the world?

---

[2] Reverend John A. Treinen, CSsR. (1906–1973), a Redemptorist priest and mission preacher who served at the author's parish in her hometown of St. Louis, Missouri. He was a spiritual guide to her in her formative years and encouraged her in her religious vocation. He visited the Roswell monastery in the early 1970s.—ED.

Friendship depends on union and communion. Therefore, as concerns religious communities, if there is not union
in essentials, there is no community. Now, I don't mean at
all that everybody has to think alike; in fact, I mean quite
the opposite. Just recently I had what I consider a very
rewarding experience. One of the community sisters came
to talk over with me a point on which I feel quite strongly
but which is certainly not of the essence of our life. She
didn't feel the same way. We talked about it at some length.
Well, it isn't important what the point was. The thing that
I consider important is that she felt perfectly free to come
and say what she thought. If she felt that she could not tell
me her real feelings on the point, I think that this would
be a very sad state of affairs in religious life.

It shows a great lack of capacity for friendship and for
spiritual growth as well as great psychic immaturity if I am
not able to bear opposite opinions. As concerns religious
life, you have to have agreement on essentials. I am not
contradicting what I just said! If we do not agree on essentials and if we do not have real love for one another, then
we are not a community; we are a hoax, we are phoney,
we have nothing to build on. However, given these things,
given a common goal, a real unity on all that is essential,
and, above all, a real love for one another, then we have
the beginnings of the maturity that can afford to disagree
on other things and is, in fact, enriched by differences.

You see what an impoverishment it would be if we all
felt and thought the same on everything. Suppose every
sister here had the same favorite author, everyone had the
same favorite poem, the same favorite piece of music. To
agree to live in community does not mean that everyone
has to have the same favorite color. These are ridiculous
examples, of course; but there has been in some areas in

the past a community "ideal" achieved by taking the person and pushing her into this "community form". Everyone was to come out the same little figure with sweet little buttons, like the cookies we make for Saint Nicholas' day. Perhaps life would be a lot simpler that way, but certainly not as interesting. And I'm glad that I haven't noticed it around here. I certainly know you one from the other, and I do not discover—thank God—two of any one kind.

Now, whereas in the past there may have been a lack of friendship, a lack of communication, a lack of desire to let the individual be herself, we presently have the other extreme mentioned before—an attack upon individuality in an entirely different way than pushing for uniformity. We are talking a great deal about the individual and at the same time denying her in many areas, like privacy. Interestingly, there has come out a long screed in the United States Congressional Record against sensitivity sessions. A strange place to find the denouncement, isn't it? A lengthy address was made by a congressman, and then there was a counteraddress condemning this procedure as brainwashing and detailing what harm it is doing. Someone mailed it to us, and I shall have it read at table.

We are to be available to one another. This is essential to religious friendship; but we are not to invade one another. No one has this right. A superior has not a right to invade a sister's interior privacy, and certainly sister and sister have not the right to invade each other. "What are you thinking?" "What is your prayer about?" "What is God saying to you?" I know that some communities are energetically engaged in this type of interchange now, thinking that it is a good thing; but I tell you, dear sisters, it is a very bad thing and has very bad results because this is not the way God created human nature to be.

God himself respects the privacy of the person. And what she is enabled by love, because she *is* loved and approved, and what she *wishes* to reveal of herself is a beautiful thing. Out of this can come warm spontaneous sharings, spontaneous prayer at times, and deep interpersonal relationships; but these things grow, and they come naturally. They cannot be forced, they cannot be mechanized, and they cannot, above all, be made artificial.

We spoke of discovering ourselves better in community than in isolation. We want to remember that this is a normal process, a natural unfolding. Sometimes we see the opposite stance taken. We have perhaps never talked so much about being a human person as today, as though this were the tremendous revelation in our times. Well, I always figured I was one anyway, even though it seems to be a generally new discovery today. I don't know what we were supposed to have been before this—perhaps thwarted human beings, perhaps warped human beings; but you just can't get away from the fact that we have been human beings right along. What we want to be concerned with is the growth of the human person, not establishing her as a fact. She's there, that's all. And we want to be concerned with unfolding, not invasion; with understanding, not analysis and dissection.

There is a great furor in some quarters of the institutional Church these days about domineering superiors who prevent religious from being human beings. I am not at all sure how you could do that, though I am likewise convinced that you can assuredly stamp out expressions of humanness if you want to put your mind to anything like that. But, to return to the point of these "domineering superiors", may they become extinct! I am not for them; I am on the opposition, too. However, I am surprised to note how this very real evil seems almost never to be pursued to its root cause. Who is the domineering superior? She is a very insecure person who is unsure of her own authority, and, especially, unable to accept it. And so she must domineer. She is really governed by personal fear. First of all, she does not believe in the grace of office that gives her the ability to guide and lead other people if she keeps her own channels uncluttered so that God can get through. This type of person must domineer because she is unable to explain, to guide, to listen, to relate to other persons. So, far from being a strong person whom we have to temper, this is a very weak person on whom we must have compassion. Many of the things that are being said and written now about abuses of the past are quite right, dear sisters; but they are often enough not traced to root causes.

All this relates to friendship, you see. If we are to help a human being (and superiors belong in that category, too, however surprising this idea may seem to some), we have to be a friend to her. You have never been squashed as some young religious have been (or, if you think you have been, you seem to be remarkably resilient!), but remember what I am saying. Domineering superiors or non-superiors need a lot of compassion, for they are very weak and very needy. We have to respond to a need where we find it and in whatever guise we find it. And we want to respond according to what the other needs, not according to what we have decided she ought to need.

When we were listening to the commentary on the Book of Job yesterday, I was struck by how many of those thoughts of Job and his trials applied to what we have been talking about in regard to friendship, about how we get to know one another so that we can be friends to one another, and how we establish and maintain this relationship in the cloister. One thought that struck me with particular impact was how the three friends of Job blinded themselves as to how they could really help him, by making snap judgments. Remember how they really came with love, how they really came with charity, how they came as true friends of Job.

Anyone who has the least stirrings of poetry in her soul, and certainly every contemplative has, cannot help being moved by the poetic way this is expressed in the Book of Job. When his friends saw how great his sufferings were, they sat seven days and nights beside him, uttering not a word. Well, now, let's stop right there for a moment. How can we have a "problem" about the idea of friendship with one another in a silent cloister? These men saw the suffering of their friend, and the best expression of their compassionate friendship was that they sat seven days and seven nights and said not a word to him. So deep was the communication of their sympathy for him in his plight that they had the delicacy to realize that there were no words for it, that words would only have demeaned what they wanted to convey to him. So, maybe any supposed problem about friendship in a life of silence isn't as big as we thought it was. But that is just a ramification of the thought.

The main thought that I was running down there is that they came with a good intention. Then, however, they took it upon themselves to analyze Job's troubles; and they made a snap judgment from which they could not be budged. They *decided* what was wrong with Job; and from that point on, once they closed themselves off from the reality of the situation that was part of God's mystery, they reduced their friendship to analysis of their friend whom they were no longer able even to see. Gradually the three men who had come with such love and had put themselves out to come from afar changed into a debate team to refute and castigate Job.

They had brought the sacrifice of love, setting down their business and travelling from a distance because somebody needed them. Yes, they had come with sacrifice, which is an essential ingredient of friendship. They came also with delicacy, saying not a word for seven days and seven nights. And that is another requirement of friendship: sensitiveness and refinement of spirit. They came all prepared, but once they reduced this friendship to a cold analysis of their friend in his situation, they closed themselves off from the mystery of their friend and the mystery of God working in their friend. Then they could not go forward. From that excellent beginning they had made, they became in the end cruelly uncharitable toward Job. Sympathizing friends ended up as the severest of judges. First they made the snap judgment, then they analyzed the situation and convinced themselves that they understood what had happened, that they understood Job, that they had penetrated the mystery of Job in his situation. From there, friendship progressively declined.

They analyze him. And Job does not want to be analyzed. He resists their analysis, and so they progress to another form of aggression, which is to blame him. They are going to teach him. Yet, they have not the office of teacher, nor have they the office of judge. They usurp both to themselves. Then, when Job, understandably enough, resists their usurpations, they begin really to censure their friend. From being coldly analytic, they "progress" to being vitriolic. In the end, they become semihysterical in their accusations against Job. They not only make rash judgments, but absolutely baseless judgments, telling him how he turned away widows and such—things that they knew he had never done.

They had regressed to a stage where they could really pour out invective on their "friend".

Now, dear sisters, I think that this is extremely important to reflect upon. How many snap judgments do we make, without even realizing it? As I said before, no one is perfectly understood by anyone but God. Each one of you is one of God's mysteries of love. I am one, too. And if we do not begin at that point, we shall all too likely begin at the point of analysis and proceed to dissection. Thence arise the snap judgments out of which can come appalling uncharitableness. These strictures that I do not hesitate to lay down against analysis and dissection do not apply at all to the "pursuing to the roots" of which I spoke earlier in this conference. You know, to want to understand roots, we have to be *humus*, "of the earth". That's right! Humus—humble. The humble friend tries to understand and to appreciate difficult plants from the root up, not from the microscope down. And to do this, she has to make herself small. The cool analyst makes herself large, at the expense of the one being analyzed. And she tends to pass over the whole notion of mystery in God's creative love.

The thought that we are perfectly understood by God at all times is so large a thought that I feel I come right up to it, have almost got hold of it, and then it gets too large for me to grasp. Think of it, dear sisters! At every moment, God knows exactly how you feel, exactly why you react the way you do, exactly how your emotional apparatus operates or fails to operate or operates poorly. He understands how things affect you, affect you perhaps in an entirely different way than they affect anyone else in the room or the monastery. He understands the things that are very difficult for you, though perhaps not difficult at all for other people. He understands how what may be extremely joy-giving to you is perhaps just a by-the-way matter to others. He knows what arouses your extreme enthusiasm, what tempts and tries you, all that is peculiar to you. Yes, this thought is so large that we can't quite take it in: we are perfectly understood by God at all times, physically, emotionally, spiritually.

No one else *can* do this, and yet we are continually amazed that they don't. That others do not understand us perfectly never fails to take us somewhat by surprise. Nor can we quite understand why other persons are not ourselves. In a given situation, I react in one way and maybe another sister reacts differently and another manifests no reaction at all. "What's the matter with her?" I want to know. What I am really demanding is: "Why isn't she I? Why doesn't she react to joy as I do? Why isn't she as affected by this as I am? Why isn't she moved in the same way?" This is a real mystery to all of us, isn't it? The only solution is a great good humor. We have to recognize that we would all agree conceptually and in the abstract that, heavens no! I don't want everybody to be like myself! And, of course, we want diversity. Certainly we do not wish people put into a mold—and yet the surprised, "What's the matter with her?" A sister may show that she is impatient when to us it is clear that there is nothing to be impatient about. "Why isn't she I?" is what I am saying. And another sister may be excited about a particular bug she found outside, while this doesn't arouse my interest at all. "Why is she excited? Why isn't she concerned with more significant things?" There is the snap judgment. To her, this *is* significant. (And it could be a highly significant black widow spider, you know.) It reduces again to: "Why isn't she I?"

Dear sisters, whenever we have a particular difficulty in understanding our sisters, or, to say it very honestly, a particular difficulty in liking certain persons, let us begin at that point: that this is my basic problem or trouble—that this particular person is so particularly not-I. Other sisters, on occasion, may be noticeably not-I—a deficit in them, of course!—but this sister seems to be on almost every occasion not-I. So we decide that we have a major problem, we think that we don't like this person and get distressed about it and mull it over in our hearts, worry that we are uncharitable, and then enter into all kinds of detailed analyses, which make the situation worse. If only we would keep it at its basic level: I don't understand this sister; I particularly do not understand this particular sister. Now, what am I going to do about it?

First, I am going to admit goodhumoredly that she is more not-I than some other people are not-I, and that is my problem. Secondly, I decide that I am definitely not going to take this sister tenderly by the hand and say, "Let's sit down and talk this over", when what I really mean is, "Now, you sit down and explain to me why you are the way you are." This is what I meant when I talked about aggressive understanding. The friends of Job became increasingly aggressive until they were downright ugly and vitriolic.

It is not good, dear sisters, to analyze other people. The way to understand others is to be open to them, and this requires a great deal of humility. Analysis is easy for the proud, understanding is not. And humility in this has to begin with the basic premise we have been talking about: that this sister or those sisters who may seem on more occasions to understand me best are still not-I; and it is never going to fail that sometimes even the most understanding sister will not understand me. This discovery may rock me a bit if I am not building on the basic premise that no one else but me is I, and no one but God understands me perfectly. How else shall we account for the fact that some of the classic friendships in history and poetry and the very Scriptures have not been without their misunderstandings? It is not God's plan that we should be perfectly understood by another human being. In fact, it could not be so. For that would entail being the other person or being the creator of the other person. And none of us can be God.

6

Enclosure of the Heart: Open to God and to One Another

To be open to one another so that we may grow in understanding, how do we do that? How do you do that, specifically, in a monastery that is dedicated to silence in order that its members may grow in the spirit of prayer? How do we do this at such times as Advent and Lent, when the abbess has just exhorted us to be more silent than ever and then comes to tell us that Advent (or Lent) is a time par excellence to grow in friendship? Well, dear sisters, in very little ways.

I spoke last time about the refinement of understanding. How does this grow? First of all, I think, out of our relationship to God. The more we are open to God, the more we are open to one another. Open, in the routine daily events, the small daily vexations and annoyances, the little misunderstandings that are the furniture of creaturehood. These may seem at first not to have any connection with our openness to God in prayer, but they bear a vital connection. The more sensitive we become to God and what God asks of us, and the more delicate in perceiving his inspirations, the more open we are to one another and the less do we make snap judgments about one another. If our rash judgments don't seem as widescreen as the judgments of those who were at first Job's real friends, if they don't seem that spectacular and obvious, we still have to watch ourselves nonetheless. This is the right kind of introversion; this is the authentic self-study.

We do this petty judging almost by reflex if we are not careful. We think that we know just why a sister did that, we know exactly why she looked at us like that, we know just why she did a thing the way she did it. Remember that classic example in the life of Saint Thérèse of Lisieux, when she wanted so much to go to the gate to help the portress? You recall that there was a request made at recreation for somebody to assist the portress. Saint Thérèse wanted so much to do it; but then she thought that maybe somebody else wanted to do this very much also, so she just took her own good time about taking off her apron, folding it very meticulously. Obviously, that is just the way a person acts who doesn't want to do a thing.

We can see something similar and immediately arch our psychological backs and make a snap judgment. You remember that the truth of the affair was that Thérèse took her own good time about it in order to let someone else who might want to help have a chance to get in first. Yet, all the circumstantial evidence was against her. You cannot, in the courts of law, convict a person on circumstantial evidence; but we often do it out of court. It would take a really deep sense of friendship and openness to God not to make a rash judgment or even a studied judgment about a little thing like that, which could happen in any community at any time. Obviously, a person who is dragging her feet doesn't want to do the work at hand—or so say we to ourselves in the inner tribunal. And maybe this is not true at all. With

Thérèse, it was just the opposite. She wanted so much to do what was requested that she was holding back, giving the appearance of reluctance—willing to take that risk. Human nature having been the same in the time of Saint Thérèse as it is now, the "friends of Thérèse", in the same judgmental posture as the friends of Job, said, "It is plain to see that you don't want to go."

You see, these things have been occurring right along since the time of Adam and Eve—judging one another's behavior and so never being able to grow in friendship. We don't know the real truth; how do we find out? Well, anyone who really knew Saint Thérèse would have realized that this was not her style, and not because the person had talked to her by the hour but because she had been open to this young saint in the community and understood her in the full context of communal living. Such a person would have known that Saint Thérèse would not react like this. Not that the saint could not make a mistake, not that she did not have faults, but simply that this was not the way she would have acted in this particular situation.

Saint Thérèse was an impulsive person. You recall how she had to run away one time so as not to give as good as she was getting. When she got a mouthful, she had a mouthful to give back, so she took to her heels and ran. Remember how she had to sit down on the stairs because her heart was pounding so hard from holding back quite a few things that she had in mind to reply to the person who was blaming her? Her reactions were ardent! This ardor characterized her in any unexpected situation. And even if the saint had really not wanted to do that simple service at recreation, it would more have accorded with her temperament to have taken her apron off in an impatient way to show that she didn't want to go. Perhaps to toss the apron down and say something to the effect of, "All right—which way do we go?" The person who said, "Obviously, Thérèse does not want to help", was a person who had not been open to Thérèse in community and so did not know her.

Now, we cannot help observing one another's deficiencies. This is our glory in the cloister because it should teach us the greatest humility and love and warmth and understanding. It can, however, become our greatest hazard. You see, we have to learn to establish balance in there.

And that brings me to two very good questions that were asked by two of you since the last conference. The questions that come out of pondering, out of trying to seek our own answers first in prayer, are usually far more interesting, you know, than the questions we toss off without a moment's thought ourselves! Well, one question was about this matter of analyzing problems so that we can be more open to one another. The other question was about intimacy. We did talk about that before in a general way, but this question regards particularities. We do not give our deepest intimacies to a wide range of persons. If you have been given a special light in prayer, you may have a great urge to share this with someone; but obviously you don't go from one sister to another and say, "Guess what? What do you suppose God told me today?" You don't hold the floor at recreation describing your "light". You know, dear sisters, that I favor and foster "shared prayer" in the sense that at times we share our reflections. But I can tell you frankly that I think some of this present movement toward turning ourselves inside-out to all and sundry is immature and tasteless. Anyone knows that the deeper one's prayer is, the less it can be shared in words. We share our deep relationship with God and its unfolding most authentically by the calibre of our lives. We know a person of deep, contemplative prayer when we meet her. She doesn't have to explain it to us. Nor would she!

There are other kinds of intimacies, however, and your question was about a family intimacy. It is a very good practical question. Perhaps there are some particular troubles in your family at the time. "Is that wrong," you ask me, "to share one's intimacies in such matters with another sister?" "Is that what you meant about not sharing intimacies?" By no means! You have to establish your own hierarchy. And by that I definitely do not mean a little coterie of persons around you with whom alone you share such things, and always to the exclusion of all others. Rather, I mean here by "hierarchy" that reason and matter vary, and you must make prudential judgments in each instance.

Perhaps you have a sorrow in your family that nobody but the superior is aware of, and you happen to find out that another sister has a similar sorrow in her family. Well, it could be an act of sisterly love to have an exchange there. You use your own judgment—your well-formed judgment—whether it might not be helpful to share this with her. Perhaps, again, another sister has a particular problem, and you know it at the time; and you want to share with her some problem in your own present or past life or some sorrow in your family for the very good reason (not condescending at all) of helping her to see that there are other people who have problems, big ones, lots bigger maybe. This could be a real reason. Or, it could be a *real* reason, just to want to ease the burden of her sorrow with the sharing of your own similar experience.

Now, this is not establishing cliques; this is not setting up about you that little coterie of the "élite" of which I spoke, the ones to whom alone you confide such things. Maybe one intimacy of that kind you would give to another sister at an allowed time, or another to a different sister. Is that clear? Because that is an important point. And I say "at an allowed time" because I credit you with sufficient intelligence to know that we have to use those areas of free time interlaced with the prayer and work of our lives and not set up an "anytime-anyhow-anyplace" sort of sharing. What would become of the contemplative atmosphere of our monastery if there were casual interchanges going on any time at all? I have seen what has happened here and there in places where this has been tried.

I expect you to have sense enough to know by now that building up the enclosure of the heart needs real disciplining. It is a delicate and painstaking work. We would be idiots to think we could just wander about "sharing" whatever comes into our minds with no sense of discipline or of our responsibility to the whole community in maintaining an atmosphere conducive to that silence and solitude which are bought at a great price in our noisy world. We want to be spontaneous, by all means. But we want to be intelligent enough to admit that no true spontaneity is possible without long discipline. The dancer "spontaneously" leaps through the air only because she has practised for years unto exhaustion. Anyone who attempts that kind of spontaneity without previous discipline will discover that broken legs take quite a while to heal. The organist who spontaneously improvises so delightfully can do this only because she has worked arduously at playing, beginning with scales and not with sonatas. The poet whose work is so fresh and "spontaneous" has sweated for years about the shaping of words to the "unbearable accuracy".

So, no, I don't think it is wrong at all to have intimacies of that kind as long as they are controlled by the context of our lives, by a sense of balance, and by a well-formed conscience. Now is that clear? That was one sister's question.

Another question was about talking things out, analyzing things and situations as distinct from analyzing persons—about which we spoke at some length in a previous conference. Well, I can't really say yes! or no! to you, dear sisters. I can help you to form your consciences, but I cannot *be* your consciences. God forbid that I would ever try to be. Let's take an example. Suppose two sisters have had a misunderstanding and they think (usually *one* thinks!) that they really ought to talk this out. Now, how do you decide about that? It is a time for silence now, yet our holy Rule says that the sisters should nurture one another in love. And there is this little trouble between two of you. Should you sit down now and talk this out? Obviously, there are times you could not. If the novice mistress has said that you are to go to the general housecleaning, you don't puzzle over "should I sit down now and talk this out?" Sometimes circumstances make our decisions for us. However, there are other times when there are margins on the day and you could perhaps think that you should do this, that it would be a good idea to sit down and talk this out.

Well, as I say, I can't give you the answer. I can't be anyone's conscience but my own. But I will say that you have to exercise great prudence in this. You have to take a great many things into consideration, the first of which is that ordinarily little misunderstandings are aggravated by much explanation. Our love should be large enough to pass over small misunderstandings without digging about in them. We are women of the Church, with larger concerns. However, there can, of course, be exceptions. It is just that I want to mention that "ordinarily" in this context is a weighty word. In fact, I would underscore it. Women are famous, perhaps infamous, for this. That we can start out with a small problem and by discussing it, analyzing it, and airing it out in supposedly adult fashion, emerge with a tremendously big problem. We entered the discussion with a minor matter; afterward, we can hardly carry out in both arms what we balanced on one finger before.

So, dear sisters, I would say, be as simple as possible. Keep it in as few words as possible. I do not, of course, mean that in an artificial way. You cannot decide, "I am not going to say more than two sentences about this." You know that I never want to be rigid or artificial about anything. If you start out to say one sentence and twenty develop, all right. Just don't start out by saying, "We are going to get to the bottom of this." Dear sisters, we don't have to get to the bottom of everything. Reflecting back on Job and his friends, we understand that the mystery, after all, was not in Job; it was in God. The friends of Job wanted to figure out how all this happened, why he was in the situation he was in, what had he done? Then they made their own conclusions and *told* him what he had done. In the end, they were accusing him of things he had never even thought of doing. You can't get to the bottom of God. You cannot get to the bottom of God's mysteries in his ways with men. As I said, each of us is a mystery of God's creative love and his omniscient action. So we try to be as open and as accessible to one another as we can be; but we are not aggressive in our understanding. And sometimes these protracted analyses, these contrived talkings-out of things, can do a great deal more harm than good. On the other hand, a simple explanation might be the very best resource. Only, keep it limited. You don't have to take an afternoon off for it. To talk over this little misunderstanding or aggravation we don't have to be psychiatrists to one another; we need only be friends to one another, sisters to one another.

If we have been huffy to someone, it is sufficient to say, "Dear sister, I'm sorry I was so ornery this morning; it was just one of those days." You don't have to give the other sister a whole outline of how you happened to do that, what led up to it, why you said what you said, and how it must have sounded, and that you really meant something else, and what five factors produced it and what ten factors followed out of it. All you have to say is, "I am really sorry that I was huffy."

Another way to approach understanding is to reflect that it relates again to this delicacy, to this sense of mystery. Why is the sister who seemed so friendly and understanding yesterday so withdrawn today? Well, maybe it is none of your business. No superior should analyze every expression of her sisters. A superior should be available, but she should not pursue the sisters down every daily lane of life; her breath should not be always hot on their necks trying to find out what's the matter every time the clock strikes. She should just be available, that's all. Sometimes the abbess will ask when she judges it well, but she won't be forever pursuing the sisters with her understanding-tool-kit. Very rarely do you do well to pursue one another with "understanding". And if a sister is out of sorts, well, learn to be open to her weakness. Simply make nothing of it, except to whisper a loving prayer for her in your heart. Women are adept at making much of little things. We can also turn this wonderful talent around and know when it is better to make very little of certain things.

You know that we can also in "preserving silence"—the wrong kind of silence—let a sister know that she is offending us, that we are put out by her behavior, that she is really trying us at the moment, without ever saying a word to her. Some psychologists are getting excited to book-length extent about nonverbal communication. Women have been experts in this from the beginning. Cloistered nuns will quite naturally grow in this expertise for wonderful good and family warmth, or for ill. Actually, it might be better for our state of soul if we said out loud, "You old unripe persimmon, you!" For, doubtless, five minutes later we would be very sorry for this, sorry enough to say to the Father confessor, "I spoke unkindly." But we can play this little record inside us without knowing and realizing how much more deeply uncharitable we are in our blame-worthy "silence".

We are, all of us, on occasion, moody. You never know how diligently a sister may be trying to control herself. Let the poor soul alone for a while. Often enough, by analyz-ing, we come up with conclusions that obscure our vision of reality and invite us to make rash judgments. This can happen among religious. God forbid that it should happen here, but I have seen it happen. A sister will make up her mind what another person's motive was, why a person does such a thing, and everything is judged out of that basic premise which may be thoroughly unsound. Then, the most innocent thing the sister may be doing becomes one more "proof" of that basic false premise.

If we always put the best possible interpretation on the acts of others, we are nearly always right and we are always happier. This is a large statement, but I hold that it is true. No one would be in this kind of society, here in a cloistered community, unless despite all her weaknesses, all her defi-ciencies, she really were striving for high holiness, unless she truly were aiming at lofty charity. The fact that her faults may be rather obvious and her crashes rather loud does not mean that her effort is any the less sincere. Perhaps the person who in public falls the oftenest, makes the loudest crashes, and raises the most dust is also, in the eyes of God, the most charitable and the most precious. Maybe she is the one who is striving most assiduously of all.

Job said some quite unfortunate things to God, but he kept rising again. Job went on struggling. He fell and he rose and he fell and he rose. He was humanity, I would say, at its comic-tragic best. One moment calling God to account and the next saying, "Never shall I open my mouth again, nor shall I utter a word again." But several minutes later, he was uttering quite a few words again. Poor Job was always struggling, so he was very precious in the eyes of God. His supposed friends were not striving; they were set in their opinions, wedded to their own judgments. And so they were not precious in the eyes of God, as God made rather clear, even though they were simply unravelling seemingly logical judgments while poor Job was lashing around. And Job, remember, had the humiliation of having started out from the apex of what was absolutely sound and right. He could have luxuriated psychologically in the fact that he was an utter failure before God because he had started out with the highest form of submission, this pure love of God. "God gave, and God has taken away—it is as simple as that, and who am I to question God?" And then he had fallen so far from that sublime height. He had begun by accepting all of God's dispositions of things, and on a pinnacle of holiness, of charity, of right thinking; then he came tumbling down from this mountain of high thought.

This is very important to remember, dear sisters, because we can torture ourselves in this way. "How did I get in this pickle I am in? How did I land in the situation I am in?" I had right concepts; I had correct theory. Maybe I started out this morning full of Advent zeal (I hope so!). Then, one little thing happened and I started rolling right down the hill until now I am lost in this anguish of remorse and self-reproach. This is what is important: What is the result of that kind of remorse, that kind of shame? Isn't it that we commit more and more and more faults? You see, if we are rolling down from the mountain of resolution, the thing to do is to get up and dust ourselves off and start climbing up again, that's all. If you sit there, rolling around, all you will do is to raise more dust. This can look like humility, especially to young sisters (not that it cannot look that way to older sisters as well); it can delude us, deceive us, because it seems a great act of abasement before God when we are rolling around in the dust and more and more dustclouds are coming up. "Oh, why did I do that! Why did I act like that? I'm not fit to live with other people!" But, at the same time that we are raising all this dust and breaking our chest bones striking our breast and repeating the refrain "I'm not fit to live with other human beings", we are actually being more obnoxious all the time. That is what this kind of remorse always effectuates. It is as though we are out to prove to ourselves the truth of what we are saying. On the other hand, to get up requires really heroic effort. Yes, it is an act of genuine heroism if we just get up and dust ourselves off and start climbing again.

7

Giving and Receiving: The Power of Kindness

There are a few points that I want to cover about the little things that go on building this friendship, this openness. Closedness of judgments stops it right away. Closedness of the snap judgment such as the friends of Job exercised, whether by reluctance to accept one another as mysteries of God whom we shall never completely penetrate or by unwillingness to admit that we have no right completely to penetrate another person's life, undermines with deadly efficacy the fragile edifice of an incipient friendship. We want, on the contrary, to build up true friendship by a continual openness and availability.

Let me give you one little example of what a trifling act of understanding without any words being spoken can mean in building up this kind of friendship, this warm atmosphere of living that each sister must enjoy in her community to know that she is secure, that she really is accepted, that she moves easily in this society of which she is an integral part. A sister must have that to grow spiritually, and each sister must impart it to all the others. That is the whole meaning of our ordinary sign of peace at Mass every morning when we place our right hand in another's left and support with our left hand another's right: giving and receiving. I give myself to my sister; I receive from her the gift of herself. If I do not give, I cannot receive. If I only give and am not open to receive, that doesn't work, either. I told you last time that all friendship is built on reciprocity, and that is what our symbolic gesture at Mass spotlights. You never just give and do not receive. That can be a very subtle form of pride, implying that I have no need of other people. I will give and give, yes; I will give counsel, give whatever. Yes, I will give and give. You meet people like this. They feel that they don't need anyone. They are the continual givers with no need to receive. That is a very insidious form of pride.

On the other hand, you have a different kind of temperament whose hands are always out for everybody's contribution without ever giving of herself to others. That is simply sloth. Both are wrong. Pride is wrong; sloth is wrong. Clear enough, hmm?

But, back to my little example of a nonverbal experience of understanding. You know that I was a postulant in an active religious Congregation until I entered the cloister of our Order. Well, when I was a precloister postulant, I experienced a public humiliation after I had been "in" at the motherhouse for a few weeks. Of course you know that when you are in your teens, public humiliations are even more tragic than when you are in your mature twenties, as you now are. And you will all agree, I am sure, that such things are very tragic even for those advanced to one score-and-plus of years! They had the custom there that after the evening study period, there was a very short spate of recreation. Then the directress would say, "Praised be Jesus Christ." And that, my dears, was when everybody stopped talking—on a dime!

I suppose some would call that directress a stern disciplinarian. I wouldn't. She insisted on discipline, yes; but it was warmed by real love, and I value her training very much. But as I saw it then, this practice seemed a quite stern procedure for a roomful of teenaged girls. Or perhaps I just did not get the idea at all. You know, a slow learner! I had been there a couple of weeks, but hadn't quite caught on that you stop talking *instanter* when the directress voiced the lauds. I simply hadn't finished what I was saying. So I concluded what I was telling this interested group I had around me, and they kept on diligently listening. I was rewarded with a quite forthright correction for this before a group of forty young persons. This was simply that directress' style of training: that if you come here and you can't discipline yourself, well, this is not the place for people who can't stop talking when it is time to stop talking. This type of formation is not exactly popular at the vocational recruitment workshops these days. Maybe there is a conclusion to be drawn from the fact that these psychologically advanced recruitment centers do not seem to be doing any recruiting. But we won't go into that!

Anyhow, I was sure that the jig was up and just hoped my family would be glad to see me next morning after I'd been bussed home. I was greatly humiliated because I had come, as all of us do, to be "the perfect postulant". All was now over, I gloomily reflected. I can still remember after all these years how humiliated I was, how embarrassed. But it was just not this directress' style to say night prayers and then call somebody quietly aside and soothe, "Now, dear, you don't seem to understand." Her style was, "Be quiet." I don't think we had as many books on psychology then, but I think her style had a point to it. It is not our own life style, but sometimes I think supposedly "advanced" directors do a little too much hand-stroking. The direct approach does have its value.

Well, there we were, leaving the study hall. And the one who was nearest the holy water font always took holy water and held out her fingers to the other, as our youthful battalion trooped out. A little postulant with straight blond hair whom I can still see after all these years handed me the holy water; and as she did, she just squeezed my finger ever so little. She never said another word about it. She didn't play superiors false and whisper, "Isn't she the ogre, though!" She did not descend to false sympathy and murmur, "You poor thing! Isn't it frightful to be treated like that in public!" She did not communicate anything except, "I understand."

We never had any discussions about it afterward, either. Yet, twenty-seven years later I still remember that little act of friendship. So you see, dear sisters, communication does not depend on words. We did not have to sit down that next day and discuss the mistress' formation methods. Dorothy did not impart any pseudocheer about how she had been through all this herself, what was the best way to react, etc. She didn't give me any lecture or any sympathy as for one wronged. But in that tiny gesture was all that needed to be said, so that all these years later I remember it. We do recall things like that, because when we are really open to one another's little or great sorrows or joys, we can show it in many different ways.

If a sister is crying and it is rather obvious from her complexion that she is not crying from joy (for we do look different when we cry from joy and when we cry from sorrow!), we do not have to corner her, wring our hands, and ask, "Oh, Sister, what is the matter? What can I do for you? What has happened?" Maybe she wants to be left alone. Perhaps if she were not so polite, she would say, "It's none of your business." But it's surely not wrong, if you are working in the same area, to squeeze her hand. And *that's all*. She knows what you mean, and you don't have to make a speech about it or propose, "If there is anything I can do for you, tell me." You are silently communicating that already. Or maybe you understand this particular sister well enough to know that she does not want her hand squeezed at that time, that the best thing with her is to act as though you just are not aware that anything is wrong—a "let's get on with the business" attitude. And if you ask me how you are going to know which response to make, I reply, by growing in prayer. That is the only way, my dears. We do not have a set of norms for friendship's expression on every occasion. We try, as women of prayer, to be open to the Holy Spirit, who will show us what to do if we allow him.

There are psychological aids to this, of course. There are sociological helps. But it reduces in the end to growing in prayer, because we cannot grow in prayer without growing in love, in real charity. Saint Teresa said that there is only one way of knowing if you are advancing in prayer, and that is how loving you are toward your sisters. If you are more charitable, more kind all the time, your prayer is all right.

The psalmist says, "Power belongs to God, and yours, O Lord, is kindness" (62:11–12). The power of God himself is kindness. And this is our power with one another. Kindness functions according as we are open to one another. No sister who enters a community has a right to keep herself for herself. If she has not brought herself to the stage where she is very determined to give herself entirely to God and community, and through the community to the whole Church and the world, then, at our daily sign of peace, if she is honest, she would have to push her sister away instead of taking her hands in the way that we do.

Now I hope that I have at least tried to answer your question about degrees of intimacy and analysis and about making decisions as to whether things should be done or not. Should we sit down and talk about this now for a while, during a time of silence? I would say in general that if you feel very much at ease with this sister and have known her for a long time, and then something has gone wrong and you feel that you would like to talk this thing over for fifteen or twenty minutes, it would be good to ask the novice mistress, "Could we really talk this thing out?" Far from being a childish request, I think that kind of asking is a sign of real young adulthood in the cloister. It is an adult decision because we have decided we cannot be sure of ourselves, and we would like an experienced opinion. It is a sure sign of immaturity to feel that we can always act without benefit of experience for which, actually, nothing else supplies—and that "nothing" includes brains and virtue.

Of course, I am not talking about free time or free days, but about a case where you really think this matter is urgent enough that you must right now, during work and silence time, talk at some length with this sister. Then, I think it's very adult to go and ask. For one thing, that brings the blessing of God with it. As a matter of fact, that is the only reason you ask. For your novice mistress is not going to say anymore than I would say to a professed sister, "What is it all about? Maybe I had better come along. What is the subject?" Rather, I would say, "Yes!" because I have such respect for a sister who does that kind of straight and mature thinking. In fact, I sometimes encourage this when there are little difficulties between sisters. It is always better if they can settle such things between themselves. But again I say, I consider it very adult for young sisters to ask, "Mother, is it all right if we go think our way out of this together?" I have never yet said, "Well, what is the topic, and where are you going, and don't you think I'd better come along and sit between you?" Of course, it might be that, knowing you well, and maybe just knowing the present situation, too, I would say that this matter might better wait a bit. Perhaps I would say, "I really don't think that's a good idea right now." Maybe I would suggest that you wait a while. Likely enough I could say, "Maybe it would be better if you would just pray about it." That is all part of being educated to form our own consciences and to become more adult in our own decision making.

I want to read to you a little passage from the book by Father Ignace Lepp that I've quoted before. You already know that he is a quite outstanding clinical psychologist and psychiatrist of our time. He begins this one passage, entitled "What Friendship Is Not", by showing how cheaply we sometimes use the term. Properly to understand the term "friendship", we must distinguish it from other human relationships, which may in some way resemble it.

> Like many other words, the term "friendship" is often terribly misused in our day. We say or write, "my dear friend" to people whom we scarcely know. Often we can say it with a certain note of condescension. A given employer readily calls his subordinates "dear friends," but would scarcely permit them to address him in the same fashion. It is common to say: "he is one of my friends" when we are speaking of someone we meet socially from time to time.
>
> As a result of this exaggerated concept of friendship many no longer realize that true friendship can exist, the kind of friendship we are speaking of in this book, which can play a decisive role in the promotion of life.[1]

[1] Ignace Lepp, *The Ways of Friendship* (New York: Macmillan, 1966), p. 39.

Now, that is the sentence that I want you to remember: "Friendship . . . can play a decisive role in the promotion of life." "Promotion" is a strong word. We are not talking about the amiability of life or the ease of life or the pleasant functioning of life, but the promotion of life. We are speaking of something dynamic, something calling forth our energies and energizing us in return. Father Lepp is implying that life does not really grow as it should except in an atmosphere of friendship. How do we establish this atmosphere? Well, we have looked at some ways already, and we shall look at a few more now.

I was quite struck in reciting the psalms at Matins this morning by the way (as we have often noted before) that certain verses leap out at you at different times. They were always there, but suddenly you discover them there! Thus this simple verse, simple and yet quite astonishing, invites us little human beings to call God blessed because he bears our burdens day after day. There are many verses in the psalms that let us call out that God is blessed because of his magnificence, because of his glory, because of his omnipotence; but this is so human, so domestic a verse of the psalms that we could say it was caught from the inmost prayer life of the psalmist. It is extremely personal. Blessed be God! Why? Because every day he bears our burdens, never gets disgusted with us, never despairs of us. God so excels our own love of ourselves that he never gets discouraged with us, no matter how discouraged we may be with ourselves. He will not give up his ambitions for our growth, for our holiness, for our happiness. And so in chorus we are all called upon by the Church to say officially in her name, "Blessed be God because he bears our burdens day after day" (Ps 68:19).

That "day after day" is a most precious phrase, because if he just bore our burdens on occasion, or if God at certain times were merciful to us, it would still be marvellous, but not heartbreaking. There is a tremendous weight of human psychology packed into that one verse and a great deal of humility, if we are aware of what we are saying. In that verse, we are admitting that God has to do this Monday, Tuesday, and through Saturday. And from us, from bearing our burdens, God allows himself no Sabbath. A Sabbath in our creation, yes; but no Sabbath in our redemption, in our sanctification. Neither should we allow ourselves Sabbaths in contributing to the sanctification and the growth of our sisters.

The understanding that we have been talking about is very directly related to the promotion of life. Through knowledge of another person, we discover something lovable in the person. I have always been amazed that in the autobiography of Saint Thérèse of Lisieux, she speaks of that sister in whom she could find absolutely nothing lovable. I think it must have been a particular trial reserved for a saint. I myself have never come across any human being in whom I could discover nothing lovable at all. Through knowledge, we discover something lovable *in* the person; and then we have a basis to discover that the *person* is lovable. The inverse of that is the humiliating fact of the kind of things that occasion in us little feelings of dislike. We tend to think of dislike for certain people, but what we usually mean is dislike for specific things *about* people.

A priest-friend and I were discussing this recently—the sometimes intuitive liking for a person or what we think is an intuitive dislike for a person. We agreed that it is very humiliating how things about people can jar us so. Father was standing looking out the window, and he said, "Isn't that true! There is that man walking down the street. I have no idea who he is, but I don't like the way he wears his hat." He added, "Immediately I am conditioned to dislike the man, whereas this is the only thing I know about the person. I don't know his name; I don't know where he is going; I don't know his position in life or his views—but I definitely don't like the way he wears his hat."

This is one of the humiliating truths of our creature-hood, and I think the only remedy is divine humor. How perfectly ridiculous this is! But what isn't humorous at all of itself, yet needs to be treated with humor and humility, is that we can allow such ridiculous things to pass over into what we will accept as a dislike of a person or at least as a feeling that we cannot ever understand that person. We decide that we just don't understand her. Period. That's it. And we close the door. So, we will reserve our energies for people whom we can understand.

Now, dear sisters, it is very true that in a given situation we often cannot understand one another. I spoke about that at the very beginning, how we are not supposed to set out with aggressive understanding. May God deliver us from people who pursue us with understanding, who are going to understand us whether we like it or not! Sometimes we would prefer not to be understood in some of our less win-some moments. What we want to do is to establish this atmosphere of understanding. And I would like you to remember that there is a very great difference between under-standing as regards atmosphere and area, and understanding a person or a person in a given situation—a very big dif-ference. The second we cannot fully control. There are some things about one another that are solely God's business to understand. As I said last time, God alone understands us perfectly, and that is a lovely thing to think about for the rest of our lives. However, although sometimes we cannot understand, and at other times are not even allowed by God to understand, we do have it within our power to build up this atmosphere of understanding. And we can do this in very little ways. Women should exercise and mature their natural adeptness for establishing an atmosphere of genial understanding and warmth, not atmospheres of tension. For we are all well equipped to do that, too. It is the same energy, either way. This is again part of your liberty that no one else can direct for you or use for you. It is your decision, the exercise of your personal autonomy.

8

Building and Dwelling in an Atmosphere of Love

We are obliged to give a good example to one another. This is really an obligation, a responsibility in community. But, dear sisters, if there is one thing that is particularly calculated not to promote growth in community, not to establish an atmosphere of understanding and genial friendship, it is aggressive good example—if you know what I mean. There is in all of us this tendency to react to aggressive "good example" by going the exemplars one better yet. If someone is pointing out by her choleric virtue that we are doing the wrong thing, there is some devilish strain in each one of us that tends to respond by doing worse than we were doing before. This is a common reaction to "aggressive good example".

Now, suppose two sisters are in the novitiate and get carried away into talking in a recreational way when this is a time of silence. Another sister comes in, and she realizes that she has a responsibility. Let's say that this is an older sister (not that a younger one wouldn't have a responsibility too, but it would call for a different expression). Well, this older sister can do any number of things. She can look at the talkative sisters and hoist her eyebrows. "Recreational talking in time of silence", comment the eyebrows. She hasn't said a word, but she has registered disapproving superiority. She may not even do that—maybe only looks at them and tightens her lips in a prim way. Or she may glance at the clock and then go very deliberately to her own place, take out her work, and sit down with "virtue" exuding from every pore. Well, she is giving an aggressive good example, and if these other sisters are normal sinners, something in their interior is going to want to say to her, "Hssst!" The sooner we recognize this little devilish strain in ourselves, the better.

On the other hand, this sister doesn't have to come in and think, "I can't let them think that I am better than they are", and so she will draw up a chair and say, "Well, pals, what's it all about?" What she can do is come in, and in a completely unartificial way that doesn't try to pretend, "I don't know you are here; I don't know you are talking; I am just hotly pursuing my own holiness, I'm not judging you", simply go about her business. This type of thing also can stand out like antennae. You know what I mean. "It's perfectly obvious that you are doing the wrong thing, but I will not judge. I am too holy to do that." Women can do these nasty little things, which are very harmful in the aggregate in community. But the sister can come in, simply smile at the two sisters, acknowledging their presence, and go about her business. Ninety-nine times out of a hundred this is the thing which will immediately bring to the mind of the little sinners there that their occupation is not the work to be pursued at the moment. Yet, the other sister hasn't said a thing. She has not been aggressive in her good example. She hasn't been prim; she hasn't been hale-fellow-well-met. She has simply kept a warm atmosphere that doesn't question, doesn't judge, and doesn't "excuse" in a saccharine way, either. That latter is also very wounding to our proud dignity. Someone can get this across without a word that "poor little weak things, they just haven't scaled the heights; they don't even realize they are doing the wrong thing." We can be so "kind", if you know what I mean, that it is very repelling. What we want to be is kind, but we don't want to come in like we are selling kindness. This, too, has a kind of aggressiveness in it.

Now, that is just one little example. Other times it may be the better part of silence to say something. Suppose it is a little work situation where a sister has flubbed it up and has gotten something all wrong although it was clearly explained. Now we all have to work longer to get this done. Far from being an infraction of silence, it could be very sisterly just perhaps to whisper to that sister as the occasion presents itself, "Don't you feel a perfect fool when you get such clear directions wrong! But you are such a comfort to me—sometimes I think I am the only one who does that." Now this isn't artificial, because I am sure that this has happened to each of us on some occasion, that what is clear as the daylight was a fog to me. I think that to step into a sister's embarrassment with that kind of affection is part of what Holy Mother Clare means by nurturing one another. This establishes an area of friendship, and that sister is not likely to forget it. No normal person enjoys feeling foolish, feeling stupid. We may know that this is good for us in the abstract, but nobody eats it up like a chocolate soda. You wouldn't be normal if you did.

The next thing on our little agenda here is knowledge of the real person. Brushing aside the little things we tend to dislike about one another begets love. There is a beautiful chain here. Knowledge discovers something lovable *in* a person. Then, this gives us a basis for discovering that the *person* is lovable: that there is not just some lovable thing in her, that once she did something right, once she was very clever (because she agreed with me, perhaps!), or once she was very wise because she quoted something I had said. No, we discover something lovable in her that gives us the basis for understanding that she herself is lovable.

Then the next progression is that knowledge of the real person is not concerned just with something about her but with the person herself. This is what engenders love, real love, the love of friendship. Now this can be built by silent understanding, too. I gave you a little example last time of how twenty-five years later I remember pressure on my second finger by another young person. There is also the light in the eye that can mean so much either for healing or for wounding. Who of us doesn't know how we can be affected by a look, by a glance! I would really prefer a sister to fail in charity by a quick word, by a vexed word, by an expression of annoyance that will later humiliate and hopefully humble any normal sister, than that without a word she should correct, offend, judge by her eyes. This is far more wounding, far more subtle, far more proud. If a sister says something that is out of place, I would much prefer that a sister, forgetting her own spiritual poise and slipping in charity, would give back a snappy word to the other sister rather than give her a cold look. This is very much more wounding than words. Be careful of that.

Of course, that has a happy inverse. So much can be said by a ten-second locking of the eyes. How much understanding can be given when a sister has said the wrong thing! Sometimes just a meeting of eyes with warmth conveys that you are not offended. A gracious look can say a whole paragraph: "I have done this same thing. I have said things that came over like a lead balloon." All this is part of woman-liness. It is part of promoting life by friendship.

Now let us do a bit of reflecting on the matter of emotional impoverishment on which I touched before. I want to dwell a little more on that this morning because, dear sisters, we are too inclined to set that aside. Maybe we even think that there is something wrong with God's creation—that the Lord gave us a soul and a body that were very good, but then he slipped up and gave us emotions, that he made a really bad slip in some people and gave them very strong emotions. We want to get away from that negative idea and come over to the opposite.

If a sister is highly endowed intellectually everyone will acknowledge that this is a good thing, but it will likely be pointed out to her that she should guard against intellectual pride. However, it is not so likely to be pointed out to us that if we are richly endowed emotionally, this is also a very good thing and contributory toward community; but that just as we guard against pride not in a negative sense but so that the gift of high intellectual endowment may be truly and humbly used before God, so do we act with the emotional endowments we have. Now, if a sister is less endowed intellectually, it is the most normal thing in the world that in community we try to build this up. Why do we have cultural reading? Is it because every once in a while I can't figure out what to do with some time so I announce, "Well, let's read a book; it might do us some good." No, we do it simply because we really want our minds to grow. And we try to vary this reading, feeding our minds on the richness of highly endowed minds in one field or another. We need to do the same with emotion, but this is often neglected. Perhaps we are far too much occupied with reining in emotions and not enough with building up emotional strength. No one would disagree that it is a good thing to build up intellectual strength, though maybe we are too lazy to want to do it sometimes. At least we wouldn't conceptually deny that this is a good thing. But we could conceptually deny that it is a good thing to build up emotional strength. If we have persons who do not react to things, who just do not care, this is an impoverishment that must be built up in community, which must be enriched by the love of her sisters, by the understanding of her superior.

Let us go back to this atmosphere that we create. It is not a marvelous thing not to feel anything, my dears. Rather, it is something that we should remedy. Perhaps it is a great occasion of joy: you don't react. Suppose there is a message of sorrow that is communicated: you don't react. Well, dear sisters, then there is something anemic about your emotions. This is not something to confuse with poise, with recollection, or with prayerfulness—by no means! You have to take something for it. If you don't take something for physical anemia, after a while you don't have a problem with the anemia because you have ceased to be. If you don't take something for emotional anemia, then you will cease to grow as a woman. And it would be a tragedy indeed to be just walking around, a shell of a woman, without real womanly love and real womanly friendship growing stronger within us all the time.

How do we help the emotionally impoverished person? Well, not by an overcharged "I am going to draw her out" kind of thing. The person who is less equipped by nature to react to a group or to contribute to various enterprises or subjects of conversation is to be helped in a very unobtrusive, loving way, and not by setting out to help her like a kindly bulldozer. The therapy needed is much more gentle and relates most of all to this atmosphere of understanding. As I said last time, we are all mysteries, each one a separate mystery of God; and I would add to that that we are very precious mysteries of God, very fragile mysteries of God. None of us can gauge (we will know only in eternity) how we are affecting one another all the time.

There is much talk right now about interpersonal relationships. This is good because I think that this has been neglected in many areas of religious life, but I think it is sometimes presented in a very superficial way. Real interpersonal relationships are what do promote growth, and for this we have to grow in a sense of our responsibility to one another. As I have said so often, we are here to help one another to be holy; and you don't enter a community to be holy in spite of the people who are there, but with the help of the people who are there. My community should be the area in which I can always feel at ease even when I am most awkward. Part of friendship is knowing that I will always be forgiven. There's no doubt about that. And, far from encouraging us to just live willy-nilly, haphazard, without caring how many emotional bricks we throw around, because we know that we will be forgiven, the assurance begets just the opposite attitude.

Dear sisters, we are all knowledgeable about how differently we feel, and I have touched on this before at different times. We are so much conditioned by how many different things: by the way we feel physically, by our emotional state on that day, by our monthly cycle and the rise and fall of our emotions and our passions that this turning cycle brings with it, by external things, even by the weather. We just feel differently on different days. But we have to make a continuing effort to realize that all these other sisters have the same problem. Very obvious, isn't it? But, dear sisters, for really grasping it, you couldn't find a more abstruse truth. It seems like it just eludes us. We can understand how *we* are conditioned by our moods, how *we* have to struggle, how a thing we could do so easily yesterday we have to struggle to do today, how we could be so amiable last Wednesday and are so cussed on this Wednesday. And we understand that and we do one of two things: either we excuse ourselves to the full extent, which is bad, or we are extremely hard on ourselves, which is also bad. But the failure to recognize the same conditioning in our sisters is something that is there and against which we must work.

We had in today's psalms, something which struck me again with great force. You recall that the psalmist speaks very severely about the person who adds to the suffering God has entrusted to another person. It really shivers the spine, that psalm which says that God will expunge such an assailant from the book of life. He will wipe this person out who adds to the pain that God has already allowed someone to have. "He added to the pain of him whom you smote . . . expunge him from the book of the living" (Ps 69:26, 28). A terrible anathema from God.

Surely no one of us would consciously do this. If we use a physical comparison it is certainly obvious that if a sister cut her finger no one in her right mind will run and get salt to shake in it. It is true that we may have to bring a remedy that will be painful, but we wouldn't add to the pain for no reason. But we can do these things emotionally and psychologically without realizing the harm that we are doing. If the bodily cut is there, we can see it; and everything womanly in us comes forward to heal the cut. If a sister turns her ankle, we do not say, "Why don't you run into the house?" No, we help her in, because we know she can't step on the ankle. We can see the sprained ankle. But because we cannot see temptations, we cannot see inner strain, we cannot see psychical weaknesses (true, we can see their manifestations sometimes, but we cannot see emotional states), we are likely to wound one of our sisters to whom God has entrusted a particular suffering that day. As the psalmist says, God has smitten for his own reason, for his own spiritual, strengthening reason. But God is so zealous that we not add to the pain he allows, that he says, if you do, I will wipe you right off the page. If we would translate the psalms into everyday language, this is what we would have.

Dear sisters, this is something I want you to think about. It is an atmospheric awareness that you want to develop, something of the same calibre as an abiding sorrow for sin. That is the exact opposite of continually looking back and numbering my sins, remembering the conditions, being full of bitter remorse, going back over and over and over things. That doesn't produce an abiding sorrow for sins, but rather either complete discouragement or a kind of unhealthy self-depreciation or even self-hatred that locks all our human movement. An abiding sorrow for sinfulness is a deep, gentle awareness. The parallelism to the point we are speaking of now is not that we go around and say, "Sister doesn't really look like herself today and any of ten things could be the matter with her." Rather it is that we have this abiding awareness that just as we are sometimes torn and tossed interiorly, just as we are sometimes tensed and strained by circumstances at one time and not at another, just as we are sometimes conditioned by circumstances that would not affect us at another time, so are these things continually happening to these most precious mysteries of God, the sisters with whom I live.

Remember, we are drawing down this anathema of God by really wounding a sister at a time when she can't take another wound. We don't know, looking around at one another, being with one another at work, what is happening in a sister's interior. Perhaps she is having a tremendous struggle with charity in some particular aspect that day, maybe she is really having a fiery little encounter with herself over a point of obedience, maybe she is really tortured at that hour by unchaste imaginations and is raw and suffering. A lack of understanding, a roughness with that sister at that time might be just too much. And think what this could do. Now I don't want this to create any rigid alarm in you, but I do want you to try to add to your sense of womanliness, of this loving geniality, and to remember that we really can harm one another.

We have in our new Constitutions a text stating that chastity flourishes better in an atmosphere of love. Well, you can't just say that is a lovely sentence and we all believe it, but not really bring it into all the practical details of daily living. So does charity grow where charity is, and so does obedience flourish where obedience is being practiced. You see, dear sisters, we do have this tremendous responsibility for our sisters' emotional growth. If a sister is hurt at a moment when she can simply not afford another hurt, you could abort her emotional growth besides doing her spiritual harm by your lack of consideration.

It occurred to me in praying about this morning's conference, that the qualities which our Holy Mother Clare set down for the abbess particularly to cultivate in herself are also the qualities of friendship. It belongs to the atmosphere of friendship in a community, that the sisters are available to one another, that they are accessible to one another, that they are to one another a refuge in weakness.

We can build up this availability, this accessibility in many ways. How will the other sisters feel that you are available? Well, from your general manner, that is true, but sometimes by specifically showing them.

Suppose it is just a matter of physical service. You know that it is getting close to the bell for the Divine Office and you see that a sister has a lot of work to do and she is getting strained about it, which will unfit her for her prayer. Well, show yourself available. Why can't you come up to her and say, "It just happens that I have ten minutes free—would you like to have them?" And, dear sisters, when you yourself are offered something like that, accept it, receive it. What we do every morning at the sign of peace at Mass, our symbolic gesture of giving and receiving, is supposed to mean something. I have said before that sometimes we are readier to give than to receive, sometimes there are these other proud little devils in us that say, "I can do it; I can finish." Be ready to accept help from one another; then you are mutually available.

Without reasoning it through, one sister knows that another sister is aware of her small need in a certain area. Day by day we just keep on building this kind of atmosphere. Maybe some general work has been assigned and it is the kind of work in which you don't excel. So, you are getting about half as much done as the sister next to you. Now, she can show very warm charity if she has finished her allotment of that work by helping you, not in a "My dear, *I* am all finished; do you want me to help you?" way, but in the tactful, simple, warm way that love teaches. "Looks like you're not getting finished, and that is just my problem in some other kinds of work. Could I help you with this?" You see, you don't have to run around in psychological circles about it. "How can I help her,

and not let her feel that she is slow?" Just be simple, dear
sisters.

The healthiest thing in the world is to have a sense of
inferiority in certain areas. I am not talking about an inferiority *complex*. However, admission of particularized or specific inferiority is as healthy as the acceptance of qualitative
or pervasive inferiority is harmful. Have you got that? The
admission of a specific inferiority is a healthy thing. When
we say, "Guard against an inferiority complex", we don't
mean that we have to build up in every sister a conviction
that "I am very capable in all practical work; I am adept at
handling machinery; I am very talented at art." We are all
inferior in some areas, there is no doubt about it. And that
is not a matter of a complex; it is as healthy as it can be. It
is only people who are very insecure who are unwilling to
admit that they are inferior in many ways. Let me repeat
that this is very different from a pervasive inferiority complex, which is very harmful—thinking that I am just no
good, am inferior to everybody in every way. This can smell
a bit like humility, but it isn't. It is something ersatz, something that is squirted out of a can. It is not the real fra-
grance of humility, because no one could be here and grow
and thrive with a pervasive sense of total inferiority. It is
the specific kind that is very healthy. And it is perfectly
ridiculous to pretend that we are not all inferior to others
in some areas.

We are all inferior in virtue, and some are more inferior
in one virtue than in another. It would be too bad if we
were all grossly inferior in the same thing. Again, this is
part of the meaning of community. And so a person who
has not an inferiority complex, who knows there is much
good in her because God created her good, and is helped
by her sisters to realize this, to grow, not only spiritually,

intellectually, socially, but emotionally, is a sister who can afford to say, "I am very inferior in many ways", and not because this sounds good but because it is the truth. And the truth shall make you free, says the Lord. All this is part of the beauty of friendship in the mystery of community. Now, go and proclaim the mystery to one another.